How to Know the Will of God

By Knofel Staton

A Division of Standard Publishing
Cincinnati, Ohio
40-027

Dedicated
to my wife, Julia,
whose ministry to me makes
my ministry to others possible

Library of Congress Catalog Card No. 74-31673
ISBN: 0-87239-057-8

Preface

"What is the will of God for my life, and how can I know it?" I suspect that Christians have asked this question more than any other. It is encouraging that we want to know. Yet a paradox exists when many want to know God's will, but bypass the rational faculty God has given us for knowing: the mind. Perhaps this is because we do not trust our minds; but God has renewed the mind of the redeemed and wants it to be used.

To demand that God tell us precisely each daily decision we should make may be to avoid the responsibility of deciding and acting out of the freedom of our love and faith. God wants to free us to live abundantly, not to fossilize us by keeping us from moving until He snaps His fingers.

Not only do we want to know where God is in our decisions, but we also want to know where God is in our disasters. Christians have tried to understand God and sorrow in various ways. At times we are tempted to dismiss the reality of God, and at other times the reality of sorrow. We must come to grips with the reality of both. We need to know how they are related, and what responsibilities we have.

The God of many of us has been too small. We have restricted Him when He never intended to be restricted. We have programmed anxiety when He wanted to bless. We have married Him to only one decision when He would have been comfortable with any one of many. It is my prayer that the reader will become unfettered, free to live daily in the security that God is bigger than we can imagine. May this book show us the liberation in God's rich grace.

—*Knofel Staton*

Contents

PART I

God in Our Decisions

"Not my will, but thine, be done"
—Luke 22:42

Wrestling With God

"How can a person really know the will of God for his life?" This is probably the most common question that Christians ask. As I travel, I hear it from both mature Christians and new Christians, from both PhD's and high school dropouts, from both urban and rural residents, from both business executives and laborers, from both whites and blacks, from both professors and students, from both those established in their vocations and those deciding to embark upon a career.

"God, what would You have me do?" is a question we ought to ask, for God is concerned with every aspect of our lives. He is interested in everything that concerns us: our worship and work; our choice of a hobby and our choice of a "hubby." How do we discover God's will?

Some people use the "simultaneous experience" approach. I know a man who was praying for God's guidance in choosing a life's mate. While he was praying for this, the telephone rang. It was a girl calling to ask him a question about a school assignment. My friend decided that God was answering his prayer by putting into the girl's mind the idea of telephoning him. He believed that these simultaneous experiences, his praying and her telephoning, were God's doing. To him, her phone call was God's way of saying, "This is the girl I have picked out for you."

My friend immediately started a courtship with the girl, proposed marriage soon afterward, and was crushed later when it became clear that they were not meant for each other at all. Did God let him down? Would there have been any other way for him to know God's will?

The apostle Peter used this approach in Acts 10. Peter went to the housetop to pray. As he prayed he saw a vision of all kinds of food. God said to him, "Kill and eat." Peter refused. While Peter was thinking about that vision, three men came to invite him into a Gentile's house to speak (simultaneous experiences). When Peter told Cornelius the meaning of the vision, he said that God had shown him that all men were equal and that God shows no partiality.

Peter's simultaneous experiences and those of my friend were different in one major point. My friend thought he had received a revelation of new information. God did not give Peter any new information. Jesus had made it clear previously by His activities that Jews could and should have fellowship with Gentiles. Peter had heard Him say, "Make disciples of *all* nations" (Matthew 28:19; NIV). He had heard Jesus stress the fact that forgiveness of sins through Him should be preached to *all* ethnic groups (Luke 24:45-47). On the Day of Pentecost, Peter himself said, "Whoever calls on the name of the Lord shall be saved" (Acts 2:21). Peter's experiences merely emphasized what he already knew but was not applying to his life.

Others use the approach of "circumstantial evidence" to discern God's will. I have another friend who prays that if a specific set of circumstances occurs in the face of a decision, then God's will is indicated. For instance, if he wants to buy a lawn mower, he prays that a lawn mower within a certain price range will be available in specific stores. If it is, he considers this to be a sign from God that he should buy it. I have another friend who considers a purchase by comparing prices or waiting for a sale. Who is discovering God's will properly?

Some people use the "inner conviction" approach to find God's will. I have a friend who bought a used car in this way. He prayed about needing a car and then bought one because of an "inner feeling" that this was the one God would have him buy. The car turned out to be a "lemon." Should he blame God for the failure to make the right decision?

The mother of an eighteen-month-old baby used this approach to ascertain God's will. One day she beheaded her baby because "it was God's will." She was convinced that God had told her "in a vision" to do so.

Paul used this approach in Acts 16:6-10; 18:9-11; 23:11; 27:33, when God spoke to him in visions. The visions in the New Testament need close consideration. The Greek word for "vision" usually refers to something really seen, not just imagined. In all probability Paul and Cornelius actually saw angels communicating to them. But who is an angel? An angel is simply a messenger of God sent to

11

men with a divine message. In the Old Testament, angels were sometimes referred to as "men of God" (Genesis 18:2 ff; Judges 13:3, 6, 8; 1 Kings 20:28). Thus it would appear that a real person who carries a divinely inspired message from God can be called an "angel." In Matthew 11:10, for example, John was called God's messenger. When John came preaching in the wilderness to prepare the way of the Lord, people did ask him his real identity (John 1:19-23).

We have no evidence that the visions of Paul were merely "dreams." In the New Testament era (only in Matthew 1 and 2) God did communicate His will to man through dreams. Those dreams concerned the care of the physical Jesus. We have no other clear-cut "dream communication" in the New Testament. It is further significant that neither dreams nor visions in the New Testament included any act or word that was immoral, vulgar, or egocentric. Neither was there just a visual scene, but there was a verbal, audible communication taking place during each of the visions.

Some people use the "traumatic experience" as a way to know God's will. Tim Fry, Allen Ahlgrim, and myself were attending a week of religious meetings in Knoxville, Tennessee. One day we decided to use the lunch break to eat lunch quickly and then visit Johnson Bible College, which was only a few miles away. On the way to the college, we kept looking for an eating place where we could be served quickly. We could not agree on the right spot. When a place was spotted that looked promising, someone would say,

"That looks too expensive," or, "It doesn't look clean," or, "It probably would take forever to be served."

At the end of one block I noticed the sign "Mom's Cafe" and said, "Hey, let's stop here and get some home cooking." Tim, who was driving, looked to the left to see it. A second later we rammed into the back of the car ahead, which had stopped at the traffic light. Tim's little foreign car could not be driven another foot, but we were right in front of "Mom's Cafe." Now, was God trying to show us that this was the right place to eat, or was He trying to stop us from visiting Johnson Bible College? Was it God's doing at all? Perhaps it was Tim's fault for not watching the traffic!

Still others use the device, "put out the fleece," as Gideon did in Judges 6. I have tried that approach in seeking to know God's will. I was an air traffic controller at O'Hare Airport in Chicago, when I felt called to go to Bible college to prepare for the pulpit ministry. I "knew" God wanted me to be an evangelist like Billy Graham, but I had not saved any money. I was a bachelor, making a lot of money and spending it, figuring that I would have financial security in my job the rest of my life. I had purchased two new cars, some stocks and bonds, and a lot of insurance (I have never been worth so much dead). Then, wham! Suddenly I would have to resign from that secure and lucrative job to attend college.

Why? What caused me to begin to think about the pulpit ministry anyway? I had no vision or dream, but I did have an inner conviction, based upon my study of the Bible and an awareness concerning the masses of people coming and going at the airport. I was helping to direct them to physical safety on the highway and in the airplanes, but they were still lost and unsafe without Christ. I began to become dissatisfied with my vocation because I thought it lacked eternal significance.

How could I go to college? I figured out that by selling all that I could of my possessions, I would still need fifty dollars a week to get through school. It was then I put out my "fleece." I told God that I would call the college of my choice and ask if it would be possible to go to college full time and also get a job paying fifty dollars a week. If the answer were affirmative, I would know that it was His will that I go. If the answer were no, I would know that it was not His will. I called the college and was told definitely that such a thing could not be done. Was "no" really God's answer?

We all have wrestled in these ways to try to discover God's will. Are there any principles we can follow in our lives to know His will? I believe there are, and we shall consider them.

The Umbrella of God's Will

God is not playing a spiritual "hide and seek" game with us concerning His will for our lives. He does not hide His will and then watch us "seek" it throughout our lifetime. He has a will for our lives and wants us to know what that will is. There are two categories in His will that we must seek to understand, and try not to mesh them together when trying to discern His will.

God has a revealed will for all people in a general sense, and an unrevealed will for all in specific situations. His revealed will is called His universal will for us. This will governs His desires for all humans. His unrevealed will is called His particular, or specific, will for us. This will refers to the numerous specific daily decisions we must make individually, those which are unique to one's own personal situations.

These two categories of God's will are similar to the categories of desires that earthly parents have for their children. Parents have a universal will for their children, that is, what they wish for all their children. This would include good health, happiness, security, education, etc. Parents also have particular wishes for each child. They do not desire the same specific things for their children, for they recognize the uniqueness of each child. Parents do not usually buy identical clothes for all their children (particular will), although they do want all their children to be clothed (universal will). They do not try to influence their children to marry the same person, although they may wish them all to marry. Parents will probably not direct their children into the same vocation, although they want them all to work and to serve. They do not want their children to live with their families in identical houses, but they do want them all to have homes.

As long as certain Christian principles are maintained, it matters little to mature Christian parents what vocation, mate, or house each child chooses. Parents can be happy with whatever choices their children make in their particular situations. Parents can be happy when one child chooses one specific while another child chooses a different specific, as long as Christian principles are not violated, and as long as their general will is met. Parents would not be happy if the specific decisions violated their universal will. For instance, a child's choice to go naked would violate the universal will of the parents that he be clothed. A child's choice to live with a person outside of marriage would violate a Christian principle and would not please Christian parents. It is the same with God and His relationship with His children.

GOD'S UNIVERSAL WILL

There are certain things God wishes for all humans (universal will). When a choice faces us that would violate His universal will for us, there is no way that choice would be pleasing to God. In this category of His will, He desires that all persons make the same decisions, and He expects us to know His will in these areas. Expecting all people to know His will presupposes that God has already revealed His will to us.

It is quite interesting to consider the many times in the book of Romans that Paul admonishes us to know, understand, and consider. In Romans 2:18-21, we read that the Jews are to know God's will. In this context, it is the law or moral living that they are to know. Paul says time and time again, "I want you to know. I want you to understand. I do not want you to be ignorant," repeatedly asking the question, "Don't you know?" He is reminding his readers, not about the particular aspects of God's will, but His universal will. Note the examples:

"Do you not know God's kindness and forbearance and patience?" (Romans 2:4).

"Don't you know that all who have been baptized into Christ Jesus were baptized into His death?" (6:3).

"Do you not know that if you yield yourselves to anyone as obedient slaves, you are slaves of the one whom you obey?" (6:16).

"Do you not know, brethren . . . that the law is binding on a person only during his life?" (7:1; speaking of marriage).

"Do you not know that you are God's temple and God's Spirit dwells in you?" (1 Corinthians 3:16).

"Do you not know that only a little leaven will leaven the whole lump?" (5:6).

"Do you not know that the people of God will judge the world?" (6:2).

"Do you not know that we will judge angels?" (6:3; NIV).

"Do you not know that the unrighteous will not inherit the kingdom of God?" (6:9).

"Do you not know that your bodies are members of Christ himself?" (6:15; NIV).

"Do you not know that he who joins himself to a prostitute becomes one body with her?" (6:16).

"Do you not know that your body is a temple of the Holy Spirit within you, which you have from God?" (6:19).

"Do you not know that those who are employed in the temple service get their food from the temple?" (9:13). Here Paul teaches that material care for God's servants is His universal will.

"Do you not know that in a race all the runners compete, but only one receives the prize?" (9:24). Paul is teaching here that self-discipline is also the universal will of God.

Paul wrote in Ephesians 5:17 that we are to "understand what the Lord's will is" (NIV). How can we understand all that God wills for all people? God has revealed all of His universal will in the Bible. In the book of Ephesians, Paul clearly developed what God wills for all people. The key to understanding God's universal will is simply to know His Word:

"Give me understanding that I may learn thy commandments" (Psalm 119:73; RSV).

"Lead me in the path of thy commandments" (119:35; RSV).

"Through thy precepts I get understanding" (119:104; RSV).

Jesus put it this way, "If you live according to my commands, you will abide in my love" (John 15:10). Jesus' commandments did not include such things as the name of the person one is to marry or the job he should strive for. His commandments described only God's universal will.

Just what does God desire for all humans? Below is a list derived from the Scripture where the Greek word for "will" appears:

1. *God desires that all people be holy.* "It is God's will that you should be holy" (1 Thessalonians 4:3; NIV). In this verse, "be holy" is referring to sexual purity, as seen by the subsequent explanation:

"That you should avoid sexual immorality; that each of you should learn to control his own body in a way that is holy and honorable, not in passionate lust like the heathen, who do not know God; and that in this matter no one should wrong his brother or take advantage of him. The Lord will punish men for all such sins, as we have already told you and warned you. For God did not call us to be impure, but to live a holy life" (vv. 3-8; NIV).

We do not have to ask about God's will concerning sexual temptation, even though a specific situation may cause us to wonder what we should do. For instance, some suggest that one way to cure a homosexual is to have premarital sex with him. Don't fall for that line!

In his book, *Situation Ethics,* Joseph Fletcher tells of a young lady who wanted help in making a decision. She had been asked to use sex to get information from an enemy, and this information could prove valuable in saving soldiers in Korea, where her brother was stationed. A Christian need not wonder about God's will in such a matter. It is the same for all: no sexual immorality.

Being holy includes more than just sexual purity. It includes good conduct of all kinds in the midst of unbelievers. Peter makes it clear that we are not to give evil for evil, slander for slander, or malice for malice: " 'Be holy, because I am holy' " (1 Peter 1:16; NIV); "love one another" (1:22); "rid yourself of malice" (2:1); "do not repay evil for evil" (3:9; NIV); "seek peace" (3:11).

2. *God desires that all people have salvation.* God desires this in order for us to be equipped to live holy lives. Being sanctified, or made holy, not only refers to right action but also to right equipment, which comes through salvation. God wants all "to be saved and to come to a knowledge of the truth" (1 Timothy 2:4; NIV). Salvation involves both the acquittal from sins and the equipment of the Holy Spirit. It is God's presence within us that equips us to live holy lives. Paul put it this way, "I no longer live, but Christ lives in me" (Galatians 2:20; NIV). This happens when our lives are trusting in Christ's way. "The life I live in the body, I live by faith in the Son of God" (2:21; NIV).

3. *God desires that all men repent.* "He is patient with you, not wanting anyone to perish, but everyone to come to repentance" (2 Peter 3:9; NIV). When faced with the choice of accepting Jesus or not, we do not

need to ask, "What is Your will, God?" We need no special experience or right feeling to know the decision God wants us to make.

4. *God wants all ethnic, national, and class groups to be included in His family.* This is seen in the phrase, "all men," often repeated in the verses relating to salvation. It is seen in the life of Jesus, and in the actions of the church in Acts. When deciding about integration in our churches, we need not ask about God's will. That is made very clear. We know what His will is; the problem is being able to live it.

5. *God wants the unchanging character of His purpose to be known* (Hebrews 6:17). This comes by knowing His Word, living it, and communicating it. If an action violates God's character, we need no other sign to indicate whether or not it is God's will.

6. *God wants us all to manifest mercy in our lives* (Matthew 9:13; 12:7). We are to be imitators of God (Ephesians 5:1).

7. *God wants us to be thankful.* "Give thanks in all circumstances, for this is God's will for you in Christ Jesus" (1 Thessalonians 5:18; NIV). This does not mean we are to be thankful for everything. It means that we are to find something to be thankful for in any situation.

8. *God wants us to be involved in what pleases Him.* "For God is working within you, both to will and to work for His good pleasure"

(Philippians 2:13). In this context, it means to be involved in humble service.

9. *God wants us all to be His servants.* "Like slaves of Christ, doing the will of God from your heart. Serve wholeheartedly, as if you were serving the Lord, not men" (Ephesians 6:6, 7; NIV). Whatever we do we are to honor Him (Colossians 3:17). But our service will be as diverse as our specific abilities (Romans 12:4-8).

10. *God wants us to have unity.* There is one concept that summarizes all the above aspects of God's universal will: "To bring all things in heaven and on earth together under one head, even Christ" (Ephesians 1:10; NIV). The concept is unity. It is God's will that all be united in Christ and that we live like it. This calls for us to "make every effort to keep the unity" (4:3; NIV) by being "humble, gentle, patient, bearing with one another in love" (4:2). This means speaking the truth with each other, using our speech to build each other up instead of tearing each other down, being kind and forgiving, refraining from bitterness and slander, overcoming anger, and loving one another the way Christ loved us (4:25—5:2).

To put it all in a nutshell, we can say that God's universal will is clearly revealed to us in the positive and negative commands in the New Testament. God wants no flexibility among us when a decision involving His universal will is facing us. Why? Because His commands are all for our well-being and for the well-being of others.

22

FREEDOM

I used to think God was some kind of fuddy-duddy in the sky, or the bore of the party who could not stand to see anyone having fun. Every time He saw someone enjoying life, He would say, "I will take care of that. I will give a new commandment." But this is wrong. This is not God. He wants us to enjoy life abundantly. He knows what will both prevent and create that joy. Since His will is that we have the abundant life, He shares with us how to live that life with a capital "L". He wants our joy to be full, not frivolous. That's what His universal will is all about.

As long as we live within God's universal will, we have freedom; Jesus came to give us that liberty. "It is for freedom that Christ has set us free. Stand firm, then, and do not let yourselves be burdened again by a yoke of slavery" (Galatians 5:1, 2; NIV). Jesus came to take away the legalism of Judaism. God nailed it to the cross with Jesus (Colossians 2:14).

The freedom we have in Christ has boundaries. We could call it remaining under the umbrella of God's universal will. Under that umbrella, we are given many alternatives. God allows us flexibility with them as long as we do not violate His revealed will. Thus we can remain under the umbrella of His will, even though we may choose from several different alternatives.

Since most of God's will for our lives is already clearly revealed to us in the Bible, the first thing we must ask when trying to make a decision is: "Does this decision agree with or violate God's revealed will?" To answer, of course, we must know His Word and believe it. Then we must pour His revealed, universal, or general will into the hopper of the decision-making process. We must be living first of all under the umbrella of His general will. The individual's unique, specific situations in life, with their varied alternatives, must be lived with regard to that universal will of God. It can be illustrated this way:

God's universal will

holiness, salvation, repentance
all men included
God's unchanging character
mercy, thankfulness
serving and pleasing God
positive and negative commands

Specific situations

Individual decisions to be made

We will be faced with alternatives that cannot be fitted underneath that umbrella. When this happens, we must alter our choice so that it can be brought underneath it.

While God has revealed His universal will to us, now He expects us to make our own specific decisions. How can we do it? This will be considered in the chapters that follow.

God's Will in Our Decisions

God has not revealed the specific decisions we have to make, to remain within His will. A man cannot look in the index of the Bible under M for marriage to find the name of the person he should marry; nor can he look under L for location to discover where he is to live; nor can he look under V for vocation to discern what career God would have him follow. Why? Because it does not make that much difference to God. He does not withhold His blessings from us until we make the "one and only" decision that fits into His "blueprint" for us. The ideas of "one and only" decisions and God having a "blueprint" for our lives are not found in the New Testament. There is not just one person in the whole world with whom one could be happily married, or just one occupation for each of us in order to remain within God's will.

God is not playing "hide and seek" with us. He does not have hidden somewhere just one choice for us to discover. He is not peeking out from behind Heaven's curtain to see if we are "getting warm" in finding the right choice. He will not say, "Down in the salt mines of Saudi Arabia I have put the woman you should marry. I wonder if you will find her?" At the end of your life He will not say, "Oh, oh! You blew it! You never did find the right choice; time is up!"

God's will for our lives is not like a detailed roap map that shows us every turn to make. It is instead like a compass that gives us the direction toward which our lives are to be pointed. Whether we choose to serve as a dentist, lawyer, farmer, or housewife; whether we choose to go to college A or college B; or whether we choose to marry Joe or Bill, we can still remain under the umbrella of God's universal will.

David wrote, "Take delight in the Lord, and He will give you the desires of your heart" (Psalm 37:4; RSV). This verse means that if a man's goal in life is to delight God, then that desire can happen no matter what profession he chooses. Delighting the Lord was Jesus' desire. Do you think He delighted the Lord only after He embarked upon His ministry? No; He delighted the Lord and was within God's will as a child and when He was a carpenter. He certainly was not outside God's will thirty years and within it for only three years! He was within God's will both while He was healing people and while He went fishing with the disciples. He pleased God both while He was with the crowds and when He purposely withdrew from them.

I am not less within the will of God when I am sleeping than when I am speaking for Christ. I am not more or less within the will of God by teaching at Ozark Bible College than when I was teaching at Lincoln Christian Seminary. Whenever our "delight is in the Lord," God is pleased in our living out of that affirmation, whatever we do. "And whatever you do, whether in word or deed, do it all [not just one thing] in the name of the Lord Jesus, giving thanks to God the Father through him" (Colossians 3:17; NIV).

We must believe that if we are loving God and living under the umbrella of His universal will, then God is an integral part of our lives. "In all things God works for the good of those who love him, who have been called according to his purpose" (Romans 8:28; NIV). In accordance with God's purpose, we became Christians. It is also His plan to work for our good in all things, not just a "one and only" decision.

God is not so small that He can bless us in just one decision. Our God is much bigger than that. The bigness of God is precisely what Stephen preached, and what cost him his life. He declared that God cannot be restricted to one land, one building, or to one activity. God moves with us and participates with us as we are under His universal will. He travels with us in our decisions. We cannot lock Him into only one choice. This means we can make our specific decisions out of faith, love, and joy, not from trying to read a blueprint of God that He never drew up.

Sometimes it appears that we want a mindless Christianity, because we look for ways to bypass the power of our minds to make decisions. We try to make deals with God or flip a coin. I've done that before. I have said, "O.K., God, if the coin flips heads, that is what You want me to do." If the coin did not flip heads, I decided to make it two tries out of three. I was not really looking for God's will at all. I just wanted God's assurance that He was agreeing with what I had already decided to do.

We should not look for ways to detour the use of our minds in making choices about the particular decisions in our lives. God designed our minds; when we do not use them we are despising His design. A religion that is mindless is not Christianity. To reject the use of the mind is to fail at the beginning point of Christianity: "Love the Lord your God with . . . all your mind" (Matthew 22:37; NIV). God created our minds so He could reveal content to us, but not to reveal every minute decision we should make. If God had wanted that, He would have made machines that were programmable. When we do not use our minds, we are denying ourselves the humanity God has given to us. In Christ, God renewed our minds so they could be used in His service (Romans 12:2).

God has revealed His universal will to us and expects us to use our powers of discrimination to select alternatives in the particular decisions we must make daily. Most of our ignorance lies in not knowing and understanding God's universal will, while most of our anxiety comes from trying to determine God's particular will for us. The more clear God's universal will becomes to us, the more we can make specific decisions without anxiety and without guilt or fear that we made a wrong decision.

Many times our problem is the same as old Israel's problem. The people became ignorant of God's will for *all* of Israel, and this caused them to make many errors in their daily decision-making. The prophets made this quite clear. Jesus fulfilled in His life what Israel failed to do, for He knew God's universal will and applied that knowledge to His daily life. Yet He was flexible in His decisions.

It is enlightening to read through the Gospels and search for the basis Jesus used to make decisions. Did He put out a fleece as Gideon had done? Did He flip a coin? Did He pray and wait for an answer before every action? Did He go into a trance until the answer flashed across His mind? Did He wait for a special vision from Heaven? Did He wait for the right feeling? Did He consult a palm reader or a Ouija board? Did He talk with the dead? Did He consult a first-century Jeanne Dixon? Did He flip the Scripture scroll and place His finger on a verse? Did He wait for an inner voice? What motivated His actions? *The universal will of God.*

In Matthew 5:1, 2, Jesus began teaching. Why? Because He saw the crowds who needed to be taught. That was all the "prodding" He needed, for He knew that God's universal will included teaching (Luke 4:18). In Matthew 8:1 ff, Jesus healed a leper. Why? Because the leper asked Him to do so. Jesus did not get into a dither over whether or not to heal. He did not put the leper off until He got the right feeling. He knew God's universal will included healing. He simply said, "I will," and healed the leper. In Matthew 8: 14 ff, Jesus healed Peter's mother-in-law. What motivated Him to do so? He saw that she was sick. He saw a need and moved to meet that need. He did not go to the mountains to pray about it first, to discover if that was what God wanted Him to do.

In Matthew 9:10 ff, Jesus associated with hard-core dropouts. Why? Because they came to where He was, and He knew that God wanted mercy demonstrated. In Matthew 12:1 ff, He allowed His disciples to pluck corn on the Sabbath. Why? Because they were hungry. In Matthew 12:15 ff, Jesus withdrew from some people. Why? He was aware that they desired to kill Him. He used His common sense and decided it was time to get out of there! In Matthew 14:13 ff, He withdrew to be alone. Why? Because He had just heard about John's death and needed to be alone.

As Jesus was facing His final decision in Gethsemane, He prayed, "If it is possible, let this cup pass from me." If Jesus had acted on the basis of His feelings, He would not have gone to the cross. But instead of following His inner feeling, He continued to say, "Not my will, but thine, be done" (Luke 22:42; RSV). Jesus knew that God's universal will for Him included the cross.

Even though this decision conformed to God's universal will, Jesus had the freedom to make the decision himself. If He had requested them, God would have sent angels to spare Him this agony (Matthew 26:53). Jesus based His decision upon what He knew God's universal will was. In Gethsemane, Jesus let His commitment about God's will take priority over any personal feelings or inclinations to bypass death.

We do not have any record to show that Jesus taught people to withhold making daily decisions until receiving the proper revelation through prayer. Rather, He taught us to pray that we will not enter into temptation

(Matthew 26:41); that we pray for those who wrongfully use us (5:44; Luke 6:28); that we pray with forgiveness for others (Mark 11:25); and that we pray humbly for God's loving-kindness. If we pray in this manner and with this content, we will experience less anxiety about daily decisions. A consistant daily prayer life has a way to convince us of the rightness of an action. It enables us to live continually within God's revealed will and to make our daily decisions in accordance with that will. Prayer convicts us to do God's righteousness.

Rather than encouraging people to pray for a "light from Heaven" to make daily decisions, Jesus encouraged the use of the intellect to "count the cost." He sharply criticized the Jews, even though they prayed often, because they violated the revealed universal will of God. Of course, we must pray, but not in order to get out from underneath the responsibility in decision-making. Our first priority is to seek God's kingdom and His righteousness (His universal will), not to fret over particular decisions (Matthew 6:33).

Jesus had God's Spirit and He knew God's revealed universal will. He committed himself to fulfilling Scripture, and thus had peace in His decision-making. That peace can be ours also, but not unless we have His Spirit, and not if we do not know the Scripture. Much of our anxiety in decision-making could be resolved if we would spend more time knowing God's revealed will in Scripture instead of worrying about His unrevealed will.

We must make our choices with faith that God walks with us, instead of wondering if we should have made another choice. God is so much bigger than the boxes we put Him in. He can be pleased with whatever we are doing or wherever we are, providing we are not violating His universal will.

Paul experienced such a peace in decision-making. He was flexible. He could say, "I can be all things to all men" (1 Corinthians 9:22). He had the freedom to decide his traveling companions (Acts 15:38; 16:1). He changed travel plans (Romans 1:13; 2 Corinthians 1:15 ff). He was free to appeal to Caesar (Acts 25:11). He voluntarily decided not to marry (1 Corinthians 7:8), and decided whether or not he should receive pay for preaching (9:6 ff). Yet Paul lived his life in submission to God's will. He wrote, "I pray that now at last by God's will the way may be opened for me to come to you" (Romans 1:10; NIV). Paul did not get upset about when he would know God's will concerning this matter.

Paul, who lived a life of obedience, considered that whatever happened was God's will. This does not mean that just anything that happens to anyone is God's will. Paul lived his life in loving submission to God's revealed will, so he could say, "The life I live in the body, I live by faith in the Son of God" (Galatians 2:20; NIV). Paul knew by experience that God walks with a person with that kind of life. Therefore he could say, "I'll come if the Lord wills it."

This is the kind of attitude we should have. While making a decision, we need to realize or remember that God is in control of time and history. Since God is Lord of the wider circumstances, situations may change so that the goal we were seeking will not be reached. James said, "Come now, you who say, 'Today or tomorrow we will go into such and such a town, spend a year there, and engage in a profitable business.' You cannot know anything about tomorrow. What is your life? You are a mist that appears for a little while and then vanishes. Instead, you should say, 'If the Lord is willing, we shall live and we shall do this or that.' As it is, you are boasting, and all such boasting is evil. Therefore, to one who knows what is right and fails to do it, to him it is sin" (James 4:13-17). James stressed that we must recognize and accept the universal lordship of God. We do not have to keep saying the words "if the Lord wills," but we are to keep living with that humble attitude. He is Lord over factors that our decisions do not affect, matters in which we are not personally involved.

For two months I have been planning to paint the outside of our house. I have told scores of people that I planned to do so on a certain weekend. The day came, but it rained! I cannot believe that God covered four states with showers that day just to stop me from painting the house or because He is mad at me about something. I recognized that I would paint the house if God permitted. He is the Lord over the weather. No decision we make is to be made without recognizing that God is Lord over all. We are not to blame Him or scoff at Him if circumstances do not jell as we might plan or wish.

Paul spoke about his travel plans as if they were God's will, but he had the freedom to change those plans. Twice he wrote that he had changed his travel intentions and did not want people to be ignorant about it. What changed his plans? Circumstances about which he made intelligent decisions (Romans 1:13; 2 Corinthians 1:15 ff). We find a classic example of Paul's flexibility in 2 Corinthians 2:12, 13. Paul was in Ephesus, but the church at Corinth was having difficulty, and Paul was concerned about the spiritual progress of the people. He had sent Titus to Corinth to teach and had prearranged that after Titus' visit to Corinth, he and Titus would meet in Troas on an evangelistic endeavor. "The Lord had opened a door for me" (v. 12; NIV). The people were ready for evangelism. When Paul arrived at Troas, Titus was not there. Paul was so concerned about the Christians in Corinth, he left the evangelistic opportunity in Troas in order to travel closer to Corinth. There he might meet Titus on the way and learn more quickly about the Corinthian Christians (2 Corinthians 2:13). What a pastor's heart, and what flexibility!

We also have flexibility to make particular daily decisions. God does not expect to make all these decisions for us, nor does He want us to run scared because we had ten alternatives and chose alternative A instead of alternative B. It is true that the choice will make a difference to us, for it will become a part of the circumstances in life that condition our present and future situations. But it is not true that the choice makes a difference to God. He is big enough to go with us and to provide for us wherever we go, as long as we are living within His universal will. Believe this, and live abundantly, not anxiously.

Man's Will in His Decisions

God did not create us to function as automatic machines, or to act out of mere instinct, as animals do. We were created with the ability to think, rationalize, decipher, weigh, and to make intelligent decisions as well as to act on the basis of those decisions. Therefore, God's revelation to us is rational in nature. Even His revelation through nature is beamed to our rational minds. Paul wrote, "For what can be *known* about God is plain to them, because God has shown it to them. Ever since the creation of the world his invisible nature, namely, his eternal power and deity, has been *clearly perceived* in the things that have been made" (Romans 1:19, 20; RSV, italics mine).

God's super-revelation in Jesus is also beamed to our rational nature: "No one has ever seen God; the only Son, . . . he has made him *known*" (John 1:18; RSV, italics mine). God has revealed facts that we can know, understand, and then apply to our transtemporal and transcultural situations. It is true that God revealed detailed instructions in the Old Testament. The younger the nation of Israel was, the more detailed information God gave. He had not yet pulled together His

35

total will in the person of Jesus (Ephesians 1:9, 10), nor given His Spirit to enable men to apply His universal will.

There are some occasions in the New Testament when God gave specific instructions (Acts 8:26; 9:1 ff; 10:1 ff; 16:6 ff; 18:9; 27:24). This was not the norm for all of the churches, however. Instead, God inspired people to write epistles to further develop His universal will. These are to be read and discerned by rational people. The epistles do not call for clairvoyance, but for faith.

Paul called for Christians to obey the truth handed down, not to seek new revelation (1 and 2 Timothy). He even said that the Old Testament history was recorded for our example so we could know what we should and should not do (1 Corinthians 10). Peter developed the same idea (1 Peter 1:10 ff). So in Old Testament times, God intervened in some situations to give a person specific guidance in making a choice. Part of the reason He did so was to record for succeeding generations a guideline in making decisions.

The New Testament teaching is clear that our daily lives are dependent more upon our own willingness to do God's will than upon His intervention to hand-lead us through all our decisions. Jesus even rebuked people for not using their minds to make decisions about spiritual matters, while they were able to make decisions about things of nature (Matthew 16:3). The verb "will" in the New Testament is used often for man's own decision-making, which God expects to be exercised. He will not coerce us into a decision. Let us look at some examples:

36

"If you are *willing* to accept it, Elijah has come already" (Matthew 11:14).

"If you *will* enter into life, keep the commandments" (19:17).

"Whoever *will* be great, let him be your servant" (20:62 ff).

" 'How often would I have gathered your children together as a hen gathers her brood under her wings, and you *would* [willed] not!' " (Matthew 23:37; RSV).

In all of these instances, Jesus was giving others the responsibility of using their minds and exercising their God-given freedom of choice in deciding.

We see a classic example of this in the Macedonian Christians who, although deep in poverty, gave liberally to relieve the hunger of their Christian brothers in Judea. Paul records that they "gave themselves to the Lord and to us by the *will of God*" (2 Corinthians 8:5; RSV). Did he mean that somehow God coerced them to give? No! Paul prevents this conclusion by having first stated, "They gave . . . of their own *free will*" (v. 3: RSV). What is the relationship, then, between "their own free will" and "by the will of God"?

These Christians exercised their freedom in making the particular decision of whether or not to give and then how much to give. They filtered this decision through the sieve of what they knew was God's will for the hungry. They knew that God cared for the hungry, as demonstrated by the life of Jesus. They knew the truth of Matthew 25:31-46; they knew that the early church taught that feeding the hungry was within God's universal will (Acts 2:44-47; 4:32-37; 6:1-6).

With the knowledge of God's universal will, the Macedonians did not need any other special message or revelation in making a decision. They did what God wants all of us to do. They applied His revealed universal will to the particular situation out of their free and redeemed will. When Christians today realize this and act accordingly, actions will come from a heart of faith, love, and willingness. Then we will really have a loving fellowship with God.

Some people are not satisfied with this, however. Christianity always has had those who demanded special signs for dictating their decisions. In Bible times, signs were usually given because people did not believe, rather than because they did. What is needed is willingness to obey what we know of God's revealed will, not rely on signs. This always has been man's need. All the miracles God did for the Israelites were useless to change their unwillingness to follow His way. After the plagues were sent upon Egypt, they doubted (Exodus 14:12). After the miraculous crossing of the Red Sea, they did not believe they should go on (16:3). This is only a small part of the history of their negative reaction to signs.

Jesus noted that in those very places where God had done most of His miracles the people refused to repent (Matthew 11:20). In fact, He did not trust himself to those who had to have signs (John 2:23-25). We see a classic example of this when Jesus fed the five thousand. What a miracle! But the next day when Jesus said to the same crowd, "Believe in me" (John 6:29), they replied, " 'What sign do you do, that we may see, and believe you?' " (v. 30; RSV).

Are we any different? If God would come in person and tell us what to do in daily decisions, it would not make as much difference as many might think it would. You see, He did come in person, in Christ, and many did not believe. Even a person miraculously returning from the dead to tell us what to do would make little difference in our actions. A rich man once asked for that very miracle, but the answer to that request was, " 'If they do not hear Moses and the prophets, neither will they be convinced if someone should rise from the dead' " (Luke 16:31; RSV). Jesus' reply is saying to us that we must know God's will as recorded in Scripture, and then apply it to our particular decisions. This is why Jesus spent time teaching Scripture to His disciples. Even after the resurrection, He continued to teach Scripture (Luke 24:27, 44-49). He wants us to understand the Scriptures and to apply God's universal will revealed therein.

But just knowing Scripture is not enough. We need the Holy Spirit (2 Corinthians 3). God's Spirit in us is God's presence in us, His character within us (Psalms 51:11; 139:7). His Spirit is always other-oriented and is within us to enable us to be other-oriented as well, not self-oriented. So His Spirit frees us to apply God's universal will in an unselfish way. The greatest hindrance to fulfilling God's universal will is the lack of selflessness, not the lack of signs. Exalting self prevents our willingness to do God's will. The experience in the Garden of Eden tells us that. God spoke in person to Adam and Eve. That was a significant "sign" for their decision, but they sinned because of selfishness. We must be saved from selfishness, and the Holy Spirit so frees us. This is why the Holy Spirit is called the Spirit of wisdom (Ephesians 1:17-19), and why we are to seek that wisdom in making our specific situational decisions (James 1:5-8).

"Wisdom" in the New Testament does not refer to the accumulatiion of facts; it refers to moral discernment in applying those facts. Having wisdom is having God's disposition or characteristics within us as motivation and guidance in our decision-making. James clearly describes the wisdom we need (James 3:13-18):

GOD'S WISDOM IS NOT	GOD'S WISDOM IS
jealousy, envy	sincerity
selfish ambition, strife	peaceable, gentle
boasting, lying	open to reason
evil works	full of good works

Into the hopper of our decision-making process, then, along with God's universal will we must pour God's wisdom.

Is the decision being made without ulterior motives (sincere, pure), or is selfish ambition or envy a secret factor? Will the decision exude a peaceable attitude or will it be to "get even" (strife)? Will the decision express gentleness? Have you considered counsel (open to reason), or is the decision made with independent arrogance? Is the decision calculated to elevate self (boasting)? Can the decision be made with integrity and truth, without rationalizing to justify the decision? Can it be made without sham, promoting something worthwhile (good works), without violating the righteousness of God?

In many decisions we make, *why* we have chosen a certain course of action may be more important to God than *what* we have chosen. This is why our application of a godly disposition and intent (God's wisdom) to the specific decisions we make must be coupled with our considerations of God's universal will. It would be natural to add the characteristics listed in 1 Corinthians 13:4-7 and Galatians 5:22-25 to the aspects of wisdom already listed. Our chart for knowing God's will would then look like this:

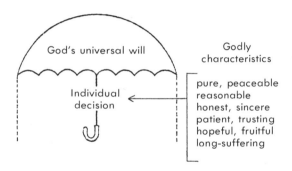

If we consider all these things in making decisions, we will be well on the way toward selecting an alternative that is pleasing to God. (Remember, any one of several alternatives may be pleasing to Him.)

In addition to considering God's characteristics and His universal will, we should also consider: general principles, our charisma, counsel from others, our feelings, our common sense, and trust. These must be undergirded with prayer and a willingness to submit the will to God. Let us examine these additional criteria:

GENERAL PRINCIPLES refer to any Biblical teaching that touches upon the specific decisions we are making. For instance, if we are making a decision about a neutral cultural issue, the general principles in 1 Corinthians 8 should be considered. This will come down to the question, "Will this offend a brother?"

CHARISMA refers to the God-given talents or abilities that we have. God does not expect us to make a decision that would violate our individual charisma. Every Christian has charisma and is to function in accordance with it (Romans 12:4-6). It is in this way that the church functions as a body. Individuals are like cells in a body, sharing their individual contribution to the whole body (1 Corinthians 12:14 ff; Ephesians 4:11-16). Any charisma we have will fall under one of the following general headings: preaching, teaching, leadership, exhortation (strengthening, encouraging), contributing in liberality, and acts of mercy (Romans 12:6-8). How do we know what our charisma is? The following guidelines should be considered:

(1) *Interest*. Are you interested in this kind of activity or work? Anything we spend time doing should excite us or hold our interest, otherwise it will be a waste of time.

(2) *Ability*. Can you do it? Is it something that you can begin and complete with efficiency and a sense of accomplishment? If so, chances are good that you will be better in this work than someone else.

(3) *Experiment*. Have you really tried to discover your charisma? Some people say, "I can't do anything," and never really try. This is a cop-out. Sometimes we discover what our charisma is by experimenting and learning (trial and error). At least this way we can learn what our charisma is not.

At one time I thought I would like to sing in a quartet. After all, doesn't everyone come to hear a quartet? No one else knew about this interest or talent of mine. So one day in college, when a friend was to lead singing in chapel, I said, "How about putting me on the program to sing a solo?" He did, and I sang, "How Great Thou Art." The congregation I was serving asked me to sing a solo, so I sang, "How Great Thou Art." Hearing that I had been singing, my mother-in-law asked me to sing for her home church when I came for a visit. I sang, "How Great Thou Art." Now, the point is this: I remained at the college for several more years; I continued serving the congregation for another year; I have made several more visits to my mother-in-law's church. No one has ever asked me to sing a solo again! I experimented, and learned what my charisma is not.

(4) *Advice*. Listen to what others say. Many times others see our abilities better than we do. When people tell you, "You would make a good teacher," do not keep saying, "No, I wouldn't." Consider it.

(5) *Satisfaction*. Do you get personal satisfaction in this kind of service? God does not want us to dislike what we do for Him. I used to think that giving my life as a personal sacrifice meant that I had to dislike what I did for

God. How can it be fun to be a sacrifice? How wrong I was! God wants His follower to be a *living* sacrifice. He wants us to be excited about our service for Him. He wants us to enjoy living. God has had enough of *dead* sacrifices. The way you present yourself as a living sacrifice (Romans 12:1) is by using your charisma (v. 6). God's charisma for you will mean you will have the time of your life!

COUNSEL from others is valuable in making decisions. No person has a monopoly on the Holy Spirit. We are not to be independent of other Christians; we are to be dependent on God and upon each other. Each Christian needs the contribution of other Christians (1 Corinthians 12:7; Romans 12:5). One charisma that some people have is the ability of advising wisely. God often counsels us through others. The writer of Proverbs said, "Where there is no guidance, a people falls; but in an abundance of counsellors there is safety" (11:14; RSV). We must not forget, however, that the "counsels of the wicked are treacherous" (12:5; RSV). We must use caution regarding the counsel of others, from this standpoint and that of ourselves. Either arrogance or a feeling of inferiority may prevent us from seeking counsel. We need to humble ourselves to sit under the feet of others.

FEELINGS AND DESIRES are important in making decisions. As it is wrong to begin here in decision-making, so it is wrong to bypass them entirely. Many people have become miserable because they thought they "should" take a certain job or perform a certain service, which they neither desired nor felt was their charisma. Therefore, feelings

44

are involved. We should not let our decisions rest upon feeling only, but our feelings must be complemented by the facts. The Christian life is to move from facts to faith to feelings, not from feelings in search of facts. Our feelings should correspond with facts, not overrule them. There have been times when I have acted upon strong intuitive compulsions, but I can do that with certainty only when I know that my intuitive insight does not violate any known criterion for decision-making. We must not wait for the right "feeling" before deciding. For instance, we do not provide for our family only when we "feel" like it. We do not take a sick baby to the doctor only when we "feel" like it. Likewise, we should not give to the church offering only when the "feeling" seems right.

While preparing this manuscript, I have received several requests, and these have ranged from helping a fellow professor move to speaking for a gathering. I made the decisions instantly, without waiting for the "feeling." In fact, the good feeling came after the decisions were made. There have been many times when I have accepted speaking engagements several months in advance. Then as the time approached I would say, "I wish I had not accepted this; I feel like staying home." If I made decisions based only on feeling, I would not fulfill many commitments.

COMMON SENSE can eliminate problems. Jesus criticized people for not using common sense concerning God's revealed will while using it in determining the weather (Matthew 16:1 ff). In a parable He praised the servant who used common sense (Luke 16:1-9). He calls for us all to use our common sense (14:28 ff), and condemns the steward who hid his common sense under pious concern (Matthew 25:24-26). Jesus himself used common sense when He did not let others dictate His activities (Luke 4:42 ff; John 2:4; 6:15; 7:3-8; Matthew 12:15).

TRUSTING GOD is an all-important factor in decision-making. We must make all our decisions trusting that God blesses us as we walk through any door with the above criteria. I doubt that God is as concerned about which door we enter as He is about *why* we chose the one we did.

The foregoing process must be undergirded with prayer, Bible study, and a willingness to obey God's will. If we do not utilize this process, upon what basis will we make our particular decisions? Jesus refused to bypass the use of His mind in favor of adopting any gimmick to decide about God's will. We need to follow His example. As people made in God's image who can enjoy the freedom in which God has called us, let us make our own decisions. May we neither imprison God nor ourselves in a box that God never intended to exist. The joy of the freedom of decision, the excitement of living out that decision, and the knowledge that God will be pleased with us are the blessings of belonging to a redeemed humanity.

Putting It All Together

From the previous discussion, the decision-making process should now look something like this:

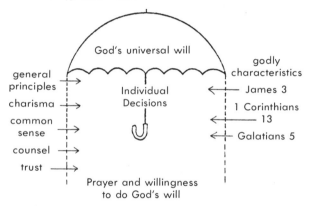

All of these aspects should be considered when making decisions, but how does this work in a practical way? Let us consider some examples.

SHOULD I MARRY? IF SO, WHOM?

In the first lesson we saw how one man determined God's choice for his mate. The only problem was that the girl did not receive the same "message" from God. God has not left us with such a shaky method as "simultaneous experience" to find a mate. Let us try using the principles that were introduced in previous lessons.

Universal Will. Is marriage within the boundaries of God's universal will? Yes.

Godly Characteristics. Can you express God's characteristics in your reason for wanting to marry, or in your choice of a mate? Is selfish ambition or retaliation part of the choice? Are you marrying someone because he or she is rich? Is the reason that the mate's talents can aid your personal advancement in some way? Are you selecting a mate out of revenge toward someone who "dropped" you, or perhaps as rebellion against parents?

General Principles. Consider the general principles in the Bible concerning marriage:

(1) Do not marry a non-Christian.

(2) The mate is to be a helper fit for you. Does this person fill in where you lack? Does he bring balance to your life? Do you complement one another? A person cannot marry everyone who is "nice," but should marry a person who is a balance to selfhood and one whose life he can complement, or complete. The place to begin in choosing a mate is understanding yourself. Can you be completely involved in an interpersonal relationship in which you must give as well as receive?

(3) A successful marriage rests upon leaving parents, cleaving to your mate, and becoming one flesh (Genesis 2:24). Are you ready for these adjustments? Can you cut the apron strings (leaving)? Can you devote yourself to the other so that no interests come between the two of you (cleaving)? Do you share

the same life goals and purpose (one flesh)?

(4) Are you ready to remain with your mate, come what may, until death separates you (Romans 7:2 ff; 1 Corinthians 7:39)?

Charisma. Does marriage fit your charisma (1 Corinthians 7:7-9)? Your sexual desires or your capability to live with satisfaction without a mate are key factors to gauge your marriage charisma.

Counsel. Have you sought counsel from others? What do others say about your future mate? What do they advise about the wisdom of marriage at this point in your life?

Common Sense. Do you really know the person? Have you been through various experiences together? Have you observed the other in his or her home environment? Just saying, "I know this is God's choice for me" is not enough. Neither is it enough to "feel" like you are in love. You cannot marry everyone you love. I fell in and out of love often during my thirty years as a bachelor. Is this the right time to get married? Will there be other new experiences you must adjust to along with the experience of marriage? These may include a new job, college, relocating, etc. Adjusting in marriage takes time. Will you have the time for it?

Feelings. How do you really feel about the person? Can you put him or her first? Can you live to please him or her? Are you satisfied with the proposed plans? Is there any feeling of apprehension? Do you really want to get married?

Trusting God. Can you marry this person with the assurance that God will bless your union? The Bible does not give us names of our future mates, but it does give guidelines to follow. Do not think there is just one person in the world you can marry in order to receive God's blessing.

WHAT PRODUCT SHOULD I BUY?

Some people pray that a certain set of circumstances will be present as a sign that God wants us to buy a certain car, house, or sewing machine. Is this enough? Since many forces are at work to manipulate circumstances, the "circumstantial evidence" approach leaves much to be desired in making the right decision. God has given us a much better approach.

Universal Will. Can we be within God's universal will and own material goods? Of course!

Godly Characteristics. Why do we want to purchase this item? Is it out of envy because someone else has one? Is it out of selfish ambition because we want to be better than others? Are we spending luxuriously out of retaliation to our mate? What is behind the desire? Is it out of a sense of need and gratitude to God for the possibility of the purchase?

General Principles. Can we own this item without it owning us? Will this item detour our love from people to things? Read Luke 12:15-21; 1 Timothy 6:10 ff. Will it enhance our love for and our dependence upon goods? We are to love people and dominate over things. Some people are not mature enough to drive a Cadillac, although they could afford it financially. Is this a needed item? Would purchasing it mean that some necessity for the family would not be provided?

Charisma. This criterion would not usually affect a purchasing decision, unless the purchase has some relationship to the functioning of your charisma. For instance, your gift of writing would have nothing to do with the purchase of a new car. Your charisma for personal evangelism or visitation could have a bearing upon your choice of a car.

Counsel. Why not ask people about the brand of the item they have and how they rate it? Check out the data in a consumer's magazine. My wife and I are planning to paint the outside of our house. I know absolutely nothing about paint, so before I purchase any paint, it would be wise to talk to people who have had some experience with paint. I read a consumer's magazine and considered their reports on different brands. Then I waited for a sale on the paint that was best. If I had bought paint just because the store had some at the price I expected to pay, I could waste money on an inferior product, and I would have to paint the house again in another year. Would this be God's way to teach me patience or perseverance? I doubt it.

We have two cars at our home. One has 133,000 miles on it, and the other has just about as much on it. A few months ago I came down with "car fever." I decided ahead of time the kind of car I wanted and the price I was willing to pay. Through a newspaper advertisement, I found the car that I "felt" had to be right one. The circumstances and the price were right; I really "felt" good about it. It was a beauty! I did think, however, that it shifted gears a bit funny. Before buying it, I decided to talk to the former owner about it.

He said he dumped it because of major transmission trouble, and the company could not fix it. If I had not talked to the former owner, I would have bought the car and could have blamed God for the mistake. Was I wrong to go against feelings and circumstances?

Common Sense. What will this purchase do to the budget? Will its use justify the purchase? Do you need it?

Feelings. Buying on feelings alone is always shaky. There is nothing wrong with buying something you desire as long as the principles of Christianity are not violated. Who would buy something he could not use or did not want?

SHOULD I CHANGE VOCATIONS?

Universal Will. Is work within the boundaries of God's universal will? Certainly!

God's Characteristics. Will the move or change of vocation express God's characteristics? Is the decision made just for selfish ambition?

Some time ago, I accepted an invitation to become the head of a department in a graduate school. I made my decision with sub-Christian motives. A few years before that invitation came, the same school would not hire me to teach in their undergraduate school because I did not have my doctorate. Now I was asked to teach at a higher level with no doctorate. Why did I decide to accept? I wanted to show them how wrong they were not to hire me the first time! Isn't that childish? I also felt I would be moving up in the world. What utter nonsense! A Christian will not be happy deciding on a vocation with such motives; I know.

General Principles. What principles does the Bible offer in such a decision?

(1) Financial considerations. Although this appears materialistic, it is not; it is realistic. Let us be honest enough to face it squarely. If the change would clearly prevent meeting the basic needs of the family, do not change jobs. A person who does not provide for his own family has disowned the faith (1 Timothy 5:8). Make sure you have the true financial picture. Consider your real needs, for you may be able to manage on much less. Of course, do not be unfaithful to the commitments you have made. Your debts must be paid, so you cannot ignore them. If you have trimmed your budget and are still short of needed income, remember that God can provide. If the projected income is so low that meeting the basic needs of the family appears unlikely, be cautious. Do not make a hasty decision. Do not confuse faith with foolishness.

(2) Commitments to your present job. Would the change break an understood commitment? God wants our word to be our bond (Matthew 5:37).

(3) Family considerations. What will moving do to the adjustment of the family members? Are there any health factors to be considered, such as climate? How about personal involvements—school and church? What about special needs of family members, such as special education for an exceptional child? What does your family desire? Why do you want the job, for the contribution you could make or just for the higher pay? It is one thing

to work for pay; it is quite another to get paid for working. We need more people who will take pride in their work, not for self-satisfaction but because of its contribution to humanity. Why not do your very best on the factory assembly line, not just for security reasons, but because someone depends on that product and cannot afford frequent repairs? "Whatever you do, work at it heartily, as for the Lord, rather than men" (Colossians 3:23).

Charisma. Does the new job fit your charisma? If the new job demands a lot of administrative duties, personal contact, or analytical work, can you do it? I know men who have been very effective in one place while ineffective in another, simply because they tackled a job that did not match their abilities. Can you use your charisma in the church in the new location?

Counsel. What kind of advice do you receive from close friends, those who can be objective? People become torn apart by weighing advice from people who are already biased. For instance, someone in the new location may want you to move, but someone in the old location wants you to stay.

Common Sense. What will this do to the health or well-being of the family? What will this do to the schooling of the children? What will this do to the place you are leaving? What will this do to your effectiveness as a servant of God? Is housing available within your means? Will your life-style be changed drastically? Is there a church in that area? If not, what do you plan to do? What would your move do to the present congregation or civic organizations you are part of? Will you be able to train others to take your place? These considerations are showing necessary care and concern for others, not just for self.

Feelings. Do you really want to move? Why do you have that feeling? Do not let your decision rest entirely on your feeling or desire. Weigh your feelings against the facts.

Trusting God. Would God approve of this move? If all the other fingers point toward the move, trust that God will bless you in it.

SHOULD I GO TO COLLEGE, OR WHICH ONE?

Universal Will. Is education within the boundaries of God's universal will? Of course.

God's Characteristics. Is your decision based upon a prestige image, or upon potential aid to your understanding? Do you want to attend college because of selfish ambition? A poor motive is the advice that used to appear on television, encouraging young people to attend college in order to raise their earning potential. Are you contemplating going just to get away from home? Are you planning to be a "prodigal son" in college? Can you live for Christ on that campus? Are you inwardly rebelling against college for some reason?

General Principles. There are no Biblical principles for selecting a college, but the Bible is full of principles about proper education. A proper education includes an acquaintance with the world, man, and God. Learning is gleaned from experience, interpersonal communication (formal education), and revelation. Can you find all this at the college you wish to attend? Is God "dead" there?

Charisma. Will the college help equip you to function with your charisma? Why spend four years in Bible college, if you want to be a lawyer?

Counsel. Why not ask alumni, college personnel, and students about the purpose, the personality, the program, the expectations, etc., of the college? Discuss your goal with the department head in your major.

Common Sense. Can you afford to attend this college? Visit the campus and sit in some of the classes. Listen to the teachers. Does the college appeal to you? Are you ready for discipline of college? Can you study well and discipline yourself? Do you budget your time and money wisely? Can you get along without Mom and Dad? Can you do your own laundry and clean your room? Can you live peaceably with those of diverse personalities and interests?

Feelings. What are your feelings? Are you afraid to try something new? Understand the reasons for your feelings. Control them, do not let them control you. Attending college is an adjustment, especially if the college is far away from home.

Recently one of our students had an acute attack of appendicitis during Freshman orientation. For a while his life was in danger. If a "traumatic experience" (feeling) had been a drawback in his deciding about college, he would have packed his bags and gone home, but he did not.

I have a personal friend who entered college to study for the ministry. He had to work to meet the financial demands. During his first semester, an elevator at the place where he worked malfunctioned. When the door opened, the elevator was not there, but he had already stepped forward without seeing the hazard. He fell to the bottom of the shaft and the elevator dropped on top of him. He was in and out of hospitals for four years. He will never be able to walk again. If he had used "traumatic experience" as a guide as to what he should do, he never would have returned to college. Instead, he believed that God's grace was sufficient. As soon as the doctors would permit it, he was back in college, studying for the ministry. Today he is a chaplain in a state mental hospital.

Just as a "traumatic experience" is not God's blueprint for us, neither should we allow a set of circumstances to dictate our decisions. I recently received a letter from a beautiful teenager, who was in the third week of her first semester at a university. She wrote about her swimming instructor, a man in his forties, who had been married for twenty years. They became good friends, and it did not take him long to learn that she was a Christian. He had begun to share his problems with her. What problems? His wife was cold to him and would not allow him to have sex with her. He said he could not go on living like that. He wants this girl to counsel him. The girl made this statement, "I feel inadequate to counsel him, but evidently the Lord thinks differently, since He has placed me here." Then she asked for my advice.

Just because we are in a situation does not mean the Lord placed us there and considers us adequate for whatever we face. Anyone with a little judgment can see immediately the potential danger this girl was in. How many other men have shared these personal things with attractive young girls of only three weeks' acquaintance? I doubt very much that this set of circumstances was God's engineering.

Doors may be shut for you to go to medical school at this time, while a Bible college will accept you, but this is no sign that God wants you to be a preacher instead of a doctor. There are many other factors to consider. You may receive four brochures about retirement settlements in one week. This does not mean that God wants you to take an early retirement. You may receive many booklets about types of life insurance; this does not mean you should buy some because this is God's way of telling you that you will die soon.

Trusting God. You may face five possible alternatives, such as five different colleges. What if you have gone through all the guidelines I have mentioned and all the alternatives look good? What does God want you to do? Chances are it makes little difference. Have you ever thought that God is giving you the freedom to choose the one *you* want? Remember, God is not a supernatural Scrooge with a perpetual, "Bah, humbug!" when He sees we are enjoying the life He has created. Choose one of the alternatives with thanksgiving that there was a choice, not with fear that you chose the wrong one. God goes with us and delights in us.

God wants us to make decisions out of love and faith. He does not want to make decisions for us. He wants us to know the joy of decision-making. This is what I learned when

I "put out the fleece" to see if I should go to college to study for the ministry. When the voice on the other end of the telephone said it would not be possible for me to go to college full-time and also earn fifty dollars a week, I put down the receiver and wondered, "How could God answer me that way?" But then I thought, "Who am I to tell God how He has to prove to me ahead of time His ability to take care of me?" I knew that preaching was within the universal will of God. I knew that I had no motives to be ashamed of. Why not step out on faith? How could I talk to others about faith if I did not have faith myself?

I resigned my job and went to college with a great desire and with faith, not a "fleece." I arrived at the college on a Saturday. I asked for a place to preach on Sunday. I was sent to Chambersburg, Illinois. After the worship service, Jim Campbell handed me a check. Can you guess the amount? Yes! Fifty dollars! I continued preaching there until a new preacher was hired. Then I preached for a small church in southern Illinois for thirty-five dollars a week, which I learned was sufficient.

At the end of that first year in college, I knew I would need to work during the summer to earn money for the next year of college. I wrote to the F.A.A. about the possibility of returning to the control tower at O'Hare Airport for the summer. I was accepted, and with a pay increase! The great thing about it was that this was the first time since aviation had been federalized that anyone was permitted to work in the control tower on a part-time basis. I learned that God could take care of me, that

He did not have to prove it in advance by answering any "fleece" I would put out in arrogance.

Now, what do we do if we know we have already made a decision in violation of Christian principles? Remember that God is a forgiving God and He can walk with us through a wrong decision as well as a right one. He did that very thing time and time again with the Israelites in the Old Testament. They failed repeatedly. God does not play spiritual monopoly with us so that when we make the wrong choice, He says, "Go to jail."

This does not mean that He approves of our actions, but it means that He has the ability to bring some good out of it, if we commit our other decisions to His principles. Admit the bad decision, recognize the wrong principles you used in making the decision, repent of them, and, if possible, change the decision to fit in with God's principles. Above all, remember that God has never been in the business of blessing people who have made only perfect decisions in the past. He is in the forgiving and accepting business. Affirm this fact and accept His acceptance of you, even though you may feel unacceptable.

CONCLUSION

God wants us to use our minds in decision-making. Learn to do so with His guidance without demanding His coercion. God delights in guiding us, but detests coercing us. Through the psalmist He said, "I will instruct you and teach you the way you should go; I will counsel you with my eye upon you. Be not like a horse or a mule, without understanding, which must be curbed with bit and bridle, else it will not keep with you" (Psalm 32:8, 9; RSV).

God has instructed and taught us through His revelation. He counsels us through the Bible, through the Holy Spirit in us, and through the Holy Spirit in others. He does not want anyone to be like a horse or mule that has to be restrained or led every step of the way. After God's universal will has been made known to us through His revelation, we must not expect God to put a bit and bridle on us to get us to make the particular decisions of life.

It is true that God can always overrule our decisions, and He is not bound to any one method of overruling. Let us not see every obstacle as His overruling power, however. When He does overrule us He will make it unavoidably clear. As long as our daily decisions do not violate His universal will, we need not fear that He will overturn our decisions.

In those areas of life God has not provided revelation, let us live as people of God willing to make our own decisions. God has graciously granted us ample equipment to use: His Word, His principles, His characteristics, charisma, His people, our own feelings, and our own common sense. Learning to discern takes some growing up, but let it be. We need more Christians who are mature.

Let us not lay God's revelation aside as if to balk at God's reason for giving it to us. The more we get into it and the more it gets into us, the more easily decisions will come, and the less despair will follow our decisions. God wants us to walk by enlightened faith, but let us do it with the characteristics of God as it was demonstrated in the life of Jesus (Philippians 2).

What we need to make the right decisions has not changed since the days of the New Testament. We need first the knowledge of God's universal will and the knowledge of God's cosmic plan that He set forth in Jesus. Then we need to take hold of the knowledge of Jesus as expressed in obedience to Him, so that we are changed in character (2 Corinthians 3:18). Then we must apply the knowledge of His Word with its general principles for daily living, and the unselfish willingness to do God's will, no strings attached.

Let us stop making God's people feel guilty or inferior if they decide to be businessmen, farmers, doctors, dentists, truck drivers, garbage collectors, or teachers. Let us allow them to know the satisfaction of "whatever you do, do it as to the Lord" (Colossians 3:17). God is not imprisoned inside one vocation or one location. Too many seminary and/or Bible college dropouts live with guilt because of us, not because of God. God has flexibility and mobility. This is one reason He wanted a movable tabernacle and not a permanent temple. Let us allow Him the mobility He himself has allowed, and live in His freedom with abundant joy!

PART II

God in Our Disasters

"But we know that God is working with all things into good to the advantage of the ones who are loving Him—those who are called in accordance with His purpose"
—Romans 8:28

Disasters and Deity

A car is filled with Christian youth on their way to a church rally. A drunk runs a red light, causing his car to collide with theirs. The drunkard walks away with barely a scratch, while all the young people are killed.

A baby is born deformed or mentally retarded. In some parts of the country children starve to death, while in other places baby food and formula become outdated on the shelves.

An earthquake, a flood, a fire, or a tornado wipes out both property and people. An airplane crashes and kills hundreds of people.

Somewhere there is a war, resulting in many casualties. We read almost daily about members of a whole family being slaughtered in their beds by an intruder.

Our land is beset hourly by personal and impersonal disasters. Why? What or who is behind them? Where is God, if there is one? If there is a God and He loves us, how can He sit back and allow such things to happen? What is God's will in such disasters? How can deity and disasters coexist?

WHO IS GOD?

What can we know about God? Can we understand God by studying our experiences, or are we to understand our experiences by studying what God had revealed about himself? This is a crucial question for us who are living in a disaster-plagued world.

To form a picture of God only by studying our experiences is to depend upon the trustworthiness of mere human rationality. To seek to understand our experiences by what we know about God's Word is to depend upon both reason and the trustworthiness of divine revelation.

Divine revelation is the unveiling of God's nature and function through His own disclosure of himself. In order to affirm the reality and nature of God, we need to consider divine revelation as well as our personal experiences, for God is beyond mere humanity. Without considering and trusting this divine revelation, humans would create their God in their own image. God would be no bigger than the thoughts of man; He would not be beyond man.

The Jehovah-God of the Bible affirms that His thoughts are greater than man's: "For my thoughts are not your thoughts, neither are your ways my ways, says the Lord. For as the heavens are higher than the earth, so are my ways higher than your ways, and my thoughts than your thoughts" (Isaiah 55:8, 9; RSV). For this reason, God has shown himself to man in many ways. The most complete way was the coming of himself in person to earth (John 1:1, 14; Hebrews 1:1-28). Jesus came making visible the invisible God (Colossians 1:15). He came to clarify misunderstandings about God (John 1:18; 14:9).

The Bible is the record of God's disclosure of

himself to mankind, but it is not an impersonal record. It is the Word of God, God's self-disclosure. What a person says reveals his qualities. The Bible is God's speech, thus revealing His qualities.

This is not to conclude that we are to disregard our suffering experiences, but neither are we to interpret God by those experiences. Instead, we are to handle those experiences through a trust in God. Picturing God merely through our experiences will lead to speculation and insecurity. Conversely, a simple trust in God will lead to understanding, endurance, and maturity of character (Romans 5:3-5; Hebrews 5:8, 9; James 1:2-4; 1 Peter 1:3-9; 4:12-19; 2 Peter 1:3-11). How do we solve the dilemma of the relationship between disasters and deity? People have taken many routes to arrive at the answer.

DENYING GOD'S GOODNESS

When some people experience tragedy, they deny the goodness of God. They say, "If evil and disaster are real, then God is not a good God." But Christ declared, "There is only one who is good" (Matthew 19:17). Amid many disasters in his life, the psalmist also could sing, "Good and upright is the Lord" (Psalm 25:8; RSV).

DENYING REALITY OF DISASTER

In the face of disaster, some people deny the reality of the evil and disaster. They say, "If God is good, then evil is not real." Mary Baker Eddy suggested that evil has no reality whatever; it is merely a mental illusion. If sin, sickness, pain, and death are understood as nothingness, they should soon disappear. How we wish that were true! Mary Baker Eddy herself died, as we all will someday. Just try to convince someone who has just lost a loved one that death is only an illusion. The disabled war veteran will hardly be helped with this explanation as he looks down on the stump where his leg once was.

In contrast to this view, the Bible shows clearly the reality of sin, sickness, pain, and death: "The wages of sin is death" (Romans 6:23). Death is not the result of an illusion. God declares that sin is a deed, not a dream. He is a fool who mocks evil (Proverbs 14:9). Jesus healed real sicknesses and disorders, not imagined ones.

DENYING REALITY OF GOD

Others, when faced with suffering, simply reject God entirely. They say the world evolved naturally and operates as a machine of nature. Whatever happens is only a natural event. God's Word says, "In the beginning God created the heaven and the earth" (Genesis 1:1). An investigation into nature itself reveals the character and reality of God: "The heavens are telling the glory of God; and the firmament is declaring His work" (Psalm 19:1). Since the creation of the world, His attributes, power and divine nature can be seen and understood by what He had made (Romans 1:20). It is the fool who says, "There is no God" (Psalm 53:1).

In all cultures, primitive and sophisticated, there is belief in God. It is unnatural to observe life and declare there is no God. The idea that there is no God is an illusion rather than the idea that there is a God. Sigmund Freud wrote that man created the idea of God because he needed a father-figure to lean upon. He had the truth turned around. Some men have created the idea that there is no God because they want to soothe their vanity and support their desire to be autonomous.

DENYING GOD'S POWER

Viewing evils all around them, some people affirm that God is real and good, but deny that He is all-powerful. They say, "If God is good, He must not have all power, because evil still exists." Nature itself declares God's power (Romans 1:20). Further, God said, "I am the Almighty God" (Genesis 17:1). The Bible is filled with declarations confirming the great power of God.

DENYING GOD'S NEARNESS

Some people keep God away from what happens upon the earth. They say that God surely did create the earth, but now He is "off doing something else." He is not personally involved with us on earth. They do not deny that He is good or powerful. They simply maintain that He is absent. In contrast to this view, God's Word says "God is . . . a very present help in trouble" (Psalm 46:1; RSV); "He is not far from each one of us, for 'In him we live and move and have our being' " (Acts 17:27, 28; RSV). God comforts us in our sufferings (2 Corinthians 1:4). Indeed, nothing can separate us from the love of God (Romans 8:38). Rather than staying away, God works good through everything (8:28).

DENYING GOD'S CHANGELESSNESS

Still others explain the relationship between disasters and deity by suggesting that God is still growing. They say He is still in the process of becoming what He will eventually be. God is evolving into a better God, just as the world is evolving into a better world. God not only helps the world get better, but the world also helps God get better as it advances in education and morality. This thinking is one of the latest fads in philosophical theology, called "process-theology." Over against this thinking is the Word of God which says that with God there is no variation or shifting shadow (James 1:17). God is the Alpha and the Omega, the beginning and the end. He is the one who was, who is, and who is to come (Revelation 1:8).

Sometimes I hear this same seed idea of process-theology from well-meaning conservative Christians. Some of them speak about a "God of law" in the Old Testament and a "God of love" in the New Testament, as if God had changed. This idea distorts the reality of God. God always has been a God of love. The Old Testament as well as the New Testament is filled with descriptions of God as love. God is as much a God of grace in the Old Testament as in the New. A study of God's dealings with the people of Israel emphasizes His grace, mercy, and loving-kindness. The New Testament does not reveal for us a changed God, but a God whose promises are being fulfilled.

That God is also a God of law is as much in the New Testament as in the Old. God's law was given to tell us how to love properly as well as to live properly. We do not find a changed God in the New Testament so much as we find a changed man. Since sin is forgiven and the Holy Spirit is present, man now has God's nature, which enables him to fulfill the intentions of God's law. He now does God's law, not because he has to, but because he wants to (Romans 5:5; 13:8-10; 2 Peter 1:3-11). "No one who is born of God will continue to sin, because God's seed remains in him; he cannot sin, because he has been born of God" (1 John 3:9; NIV).

As God allows discipline and punishment in the Old Testament, so He does in the New. His wrath has not changed. The New Testament is filled with verses that speak of God's judgment, wrath, and discipline. (See Matthew 7:21-23; 23; 25:31 ff; John 3:18, 36; Romans 1:18; 12:19; 1 Corinthians 3:16, 17; Colossians 3:6; Hebrews 2:1-3; Jude 15; Revelation 2, 3; 20:11-15).

DENYING GOODNESS IN NATURE

Other people suggest that evil and disasters are only and always the result of nature, which is in itself evil. From the beginning God said that His creation was good (Genesis 1:9, 12, 18, 21, 25, 31), and that declaration was reaffirmed centuries later (Romans 14:14, 20; Titus 1:15; Acts 10:15; Matthew 15:17-20).

DENYING MAN'S RESPONSIBILITY

Some people suggest that all evil and disasters are God's direct doing, that He wills everything. Thus if tragedy hits, God has willed it. He has caused it. This is the exact opposite of the idea that God is absent or that man is left totally to himself. This thinking says that God is making everything happen as it happens; thus man is drained from any responsibility for it. If a drunkard crashes into a car filled with Christian youth, it is God's doing, not the drunkard's. He merely became the agent of "God's will." Others go to the opposite extreme and blame the devil for all tragedy. They say, "The devil makes it all happen." But the Bible clearly teaches the responsibility of every person for his own wrong decisions and wrongdoing. The consequences of his wrong actions may affect only himself, but it can involve others, whether they are wicked or innocent.

If the dilemma of the relationship between disasters and deity cannot be solved by any of the above explanations, what is the answer? How can we have a good and all-powerful God, and yet face evil and disastrous situations? How can we have a God who is for us and live in a world that seems to be so much against us (including nature)? Where does evil come from, and how is it related to the will of God? In the following chapters we will probe these questions.

The Origin of Evil

Where has evil come from and what caused it? Many religions have tried to answer that question. The Buddha religion teaches that evil is a natural part of our makeup; thus the way to stop it is to kill desire and destroy the personality of the individual. Islam teaches that God willed evil; thus God causes everything that happens. This is fatalism.

Both ideas have infiltrated somewhat into the thinking of Christians. Those who feel that evil is the natural outgrowth of the inner man are suggesting that we can overcome evil by merely controlling our thoughts. In the name of Christianity, many people are advocating transmeditation and experiences that bypass use of the mind.

The fatalistic philosophy of Islam is suggested by some within Christianity who say that each person has his time to live and to die. When his time comes for calamity or death, he has had it, regardless of the circumstances. The person himself has no responsibility in the matter and can do nothing to change it.

Evil is the result of a rebellion against God, not the result of God's direction of people or nature. The fact that God permits evil to exist does not indicate that He desires it. His allowing evil does not mean that He planned it. It is God's desire to bring order out of chaos, not pour chaos into order.

TWO KINDS OF EVIL

Before we discuss this further, we need to recognize that there are two kinds of evil or calamity in the world. There are "personal" evils or disasters. These are caused directly by the personal wrongs of people: killing, lying, stealing, adultery, etc. There are also "impersonal" evils and calamities. These are caused by the impersonal forces of nature: earthquakes, tornadoes, fires, sickness, etc. These two categories cannot be totally separated from each other. They are definitely interrelated, as we shall see.

PREHISTORIC EVIL

It is the conclusion of many Bible students that evil existed before the history of man began. The following evidence leads to this conclusion:

(1) There was a tempter in the Garden of Eden, who lured the first woman toward evil (Genesis 3:1-7). The tempter used a lie (evil) to instigate rebellion against God (v. 4).

(2) The New Testament speaks of angels who sinned (Jude 5, 6; 2 Peter 2:4). They evidently had the ability to choose; otherwise sin would not have been possible. Angels can hear (v. 5), speak (Luke 1:13), worship (Hebrews 1:6), observe, and learn (1 Peter 1:12), as well as sin.

(3) It is believed by some that these angels who sinned form the "principalities and pow-

ers" that stand in opposition to God (Ephesians 6:12).

(4) The leader of these fallen angels is the devil (Matthew 25:41). Jesus affirms that the devil has a kingdom (12:26). The devil is called the prince or ruler of demons (Mark 3:22, 23), and the ruler (god) of this world (John 12:31). He is the ultimate source of temptation (Matthew 4:1; John 13:2). His business is to deceive (Revelation 20:8-10) as he did Eve (1 Timothy 2:14). Therefore, it is not a shot-in-the-dark belief that the devil existed before the first human beings, and was involved in their temptation through the disguise of a serpent.

If the devil existed before the first humans, then evil existed prior to man. We read "Any one who practices sin is of the devil; for the devil has been sinning from the beginning" (1 John 3:8). Jesus said, "He was a murderer from the beginning, not holding to the truth, for there is no truth in him" (John 8:44; NIV). The phrase "from the beginning" in both verses certainly could not mean from the beginning of the devil, or he could not have fallen. It means from the beginning of the earthly history of man. The devil was part of man's earthly history from the beginning. Thus he existed prior to man.

THE FALL OF SATAN

It is possible that the fall of the devil is alluded to in Isaiah 14:12-14 and in Ezekiel 28:12-18. These are only "possible" references, because the context is clear that the Isaiah passage is describing the king of Babylon, and the Ezekiel passage is describing the king of Tyre. At the same time, the language of these descriptions may be attributing to these kings the attitudes and motivations of the devil when he fell:

"How you are fallen from heaven, O Day Star, son of Dawn! How you are cut down to the ground, you who laid the nations low! You said in your heart, 'I will ascend to heaven; above the stars of God I will set my throne on high; I will sit on the mount of assembly in the far north; I will ascend above the heights of the clouds, I will make myself like the Most High' " (Isaiah 14:12-14; RSV).

" 'You were the signet of perfection, full of wisdom and perfect in beauty . . . You were blameless in your ways from the day you were created, till iniquity was found in you. In the abundance of your trade you were filled with violence, and you sinned; so I cast you as a profane thing from the mountain of God' " (Ezekiel 28:12-16; RSV).

It is clear from these two descriptions that man's sin is rooted in arrogance about self and a desire to be as God. That is precisely the temptation Satan presented to Adam and Eve: "For God knows that when you eat of it your eyes will be opened, and you will be like God, knowing good and evil" (Genesis 3:5; RSV).

Because that is the route of man's sin, it was no doubt the route of the devil's first sin. He tried to be equal with God and perhaps be His replacement, or at least be God to himself, which would be autonomy, independence, and individualism. That is why Jesus said of those who opposed Him and of those who would not love Him, "You are of your father,

Satan, and you want to do his wishes" (John 8:44).

The devil's desire is to stand against God. Jesus called the devil "the enemy" (Matthew 13:39). He is the one who has come down to this earth to turn us away from God (Revelation 12:17; Genesis 3:1 ff; Job 1). When we sinned, we became God's enemies also (Romans 8:7).

GOD'S PERMISSION

Why would God permit the devil to lure us into being enemies of God? The answer lies in the love of God. Sounds strange, doesn't it?

Because of God's love He created us and allowed us to participate in His own image. Since God is love (1 John 4:16), He gave man the capacity to love. Man and woman were made with the ability to love God and to love each other. In order to express that love fully, there must be a choice. In order to choose, there must be an alternative. God wants us to fellowship with Him, not because we have no other choice, but because it is our choice. God will not force man to love Him. Love does not work that way. Love woos and waits; love permits the other the freedom to respond out of desire to do so.

In the Garden of Eden, God wanted man to remain in the community of unity; however, He provided an alternative for man. That alternative was the tree of the knowledge of good and evil. "Of the tree of the knowledge of good and evil you shall not eat, for in the day that you eat of it you shall die" (Genesis 2:17). The phrase, "you shall die" did not mean a physical death, but a separation from God

(Isaiah 59:2; Ephesians 2:12; 2 Thessalonians 1:9). Adam and Eve did not physically die on the day they sinned, but they had to leave the garden and be separated from God (Genesis 3:24).

We often call the tree of the knowledge of good and evil man's first temptation, but I prefer to call it man's grand opportunity. As long as Adam and Eve did not partake of the tree, they were saying to God, "Father, we are here because we want to be and because we love You, not because we have to be." But their sin broke the community of unity, for the attitude behind the sin was an anticommunity attitude. Sin is always a turning to our own way. "All we like sheep have gone astray; we have turned every one to his own way" (Isaiah 53:6; RSV). Individualism destroys the community.

God's love permitted the temptation because out of His love He made us in His own image. We are persons, not puppets. God could have made us as heavenly robots, but He did not. That was God's calculated risk, and true love always involves a risk. It is always selfless. Man takes advantage of God's love and His gift of freedom. God did not force the one and only decision on man, but He did force man to the position of making a choice.

CONSEQUENCES OF THE FIRST SIN

The consequences of man's sin were:

(1) The partnership of husband and wife turned into blame-throwing (Genesis 2:23; 3:12).

(2) Openness between them gave way to shielding their bodies from each other (3:7).

(3) Fellowship with God turned into dread of God (3:10).

(4) The need for a Savior was created (3:15).

(5) The pain in child-bearing was multiplied (3:16).

(6) There was alienation from God (3:24).

(7) Harmony within nature was destroyed (3:17-19).

Let us consider in particular the last consequence. God's creation was made with interrelated harmony (ecology). All of nature worked together within and as part of God's community of unity. The animals were not a threat to each other or to Adam and Eve. No one or no aspect of nature lived in competition, but in cooperation. There was no sickness or disease.

When one portion of His creation rebelled, the whole of creation was thrown out of balance. The community (common oneness) was destroyed. Man began to live for self and would even kill to get his own way (Genesis 4). Man went wild, and so did the animals. Vegetation was threatened by weeds and thorns. Diseases came when the perfect balance of God's creation was upset by man's decision to be autonomous.

The Bible is clear that all of creation has been subjected to a bondage of decay and is itself waiting for its liberation from the imbalance. Liberation comes to the whole creation as man lives as a son of God and not as a god himself. (Study Romans 8:18-25.) The harmonizing of creation with its potentially threatening forces depends upon humanity becoming reconciled to God. That harmonizing or liberation has already begun in the coming of God's new kingdom, but it will not be final until the end, when the rebellious humans will be separated from the obedient ones.

Until that time we will experience both good and bad. As Christians we should be pouring God's kind of life—love, peace, and harmony— into all of our relationships. We are to be as leaven, light, and salt. The consequences affect not just people but also God's entire creation. God's creation is so closely knit together that whatever the highest creature (man) does affects all creation.

The New Testament is clear that God wants to reunite all *things* under one head, not just all people (Ephesians 1:9, 10; Colossians 1:19, 20). But the reuniting of all things depends upon the reuniting of all people. God's will is that His creation return to a community of unity. Such a community can be restored only when people return to God and to each other.

Heaven will be heavenly because of the love that will be manifested by all. Disasters will not be present because God's highest creatures will not sever themselves from God. Our lives will be centered in His Son, not in ourselves. That kind of living is to invade our earth now. A taste of God's future is to be seen in man's present.

Both personal and impersonal evils and calamities began when man went His own way following the lure of Satan. This is not the whole story, however. Not all disasters and suffering are directly connected to man's sin.

The Source of Suffering

Why should calamities and sufferings be facts of life on this earth? Why do some people seem to get more than their share of suffering? Are these hard times the result of sin in our lives or in the lives of others?

SIN AND SUFFERING

Many of the Jews believed in a direct one-to-one relationship between sin and suffering. According to this view, any suffering or tragedy that hit a person was thought to be the direct response from God to that person's own sin. It was necessary, then, to discover what sin or sins were responsible and get rid of them.

This thinking was present in many other cultures. When the poisonous creature snatched Paul's hand, the natives on the island of Malta concluded that it was punishment for a murder Paul must have committed (Acts 28:1-5). In some cultures, this view was worked out in such detail that the people could identify the sin a person committed by the kind of suffering or tragedy he was experiencing.

This view of the relationship of sin and suffering raises its ugly head from time to time even within Christianity. When we feel we have been true and loyal to God, sometimes tragedy blows in overnight. We get upset or mad at God and ask, *"Why* did You do this to me, God? *What did I do* to deserve this?" Some Christians use the religious rituals and services as sort of a magic spell to keep away suffering and calamity. Some persons think that as long as they attend worship services, take Communion, and give their offerings, they should be protected from all harm.

The idea of the direct relationship of sin to suffering is the background of many of the healing services held today. If a person is sick, he is told that he has sinned and needs to repent and confess his sins. He is promised that healing will automatically occur when he does so. He is taught that all sickness is a curse, but one whose sins are forgiven will not experience that curse because Jesus took the curse upon himself.

To support this teaching, the leaders use selected verses from Deuteronomy 28:

"If you will not obey the voice of the Lord your God or be careful to do all his commandments and his statutes which I command you this day, then all these curses shall come upon you and overtake you" (v. 15; RSV). "The Lord will smite you with consumption, and with fever, inflammation, and fiery heat, . . . they shall pursue you until you perish" (v. 22; RSV).

Then they cite Galatians 3:13: "Christ redeemed us from the curse of the law, having become a curse for us—for it is written, 'Cursed be every one who hangs on a tree' " (RSV).

There are two major faults in using these verses to support such teaching. First, the verses in Deuteronomy are taken completely out of context. In this chapter God was speaking to Israel to give them guidance for entering and conquering the promised land, with no possible application to the present day. A perusal of the entire chapter will quickly make this point clear. Second, the "curse of the law" in the Galatians passage clearly refers to eternal condemnation caused by sin, not to sickness. Christ died on the cross to make it possible for us to have access to God, receive the Holy Spirit, and be justified, as seen in the rest of the Galatian letter.

Christ's death on the cross certainly did not eliminate all sickness and suffering. It is only when *all* men are reconciled to God that sickness on this earth will be eliminated. As long as any sin exists in the world, regardless of who is guilty, there will be sickness and calamities because of the resulting imbalance in nature. Sickness from that source will fall upon the just as well as the unjust.

It is true that a certain amount of suffering and tragedies are the direct result of our personal sins.

God's Word will not be broken. When He says a certain activity is wrong, then engaging in that activity will cause hurtful consequences. Sooner or later these consequences will affect the wrongdoer and perhaps others. The warning is clear, as recorded in James 3:5, 6: "The tongue is a small part of the body, but it makes great boasts. Consider what a great forest is set on fire by a small spark. The tongue also is a fire, a world of evil among the parts of the body. It corrupts the whole person, sets the whole course of his life on fire, and is itself set on fire by hell" (NIV). How true we know this to be!

But not all suffering we undergo is the result of our own sins. Some may be the result of someone else's sin. An arsonist sets a house afire, and many innocent persons are killed. A drunkard kills others in an auto accident. A wife can contract venereal disease because of her husband's sin, not her own.

Even some nationwide sufferings result from national or international policies, or decisions that violate the principles of God. The problems of economic injustice, famine, and war are often related to decisions that "miss the mark" of God's intentions for earthly living. The Bible clearly places the cause of war on the doorstep of man's selfishness: "What causes fights and quarrels among you? Don't they come from your desires that battle within you? You want something but don't get it. You kill and covet, but you cannot have what you want. You quarrel and fight. You do not have, because you do not ask God. When you ask, you do not receive, because you ask with wrong motives, that you may spend what you get on your pleasures" (James 4:1-3; NIV). God yearns to see the manifestation of His character in our decisions and deeds. He wants to see these in man individually, nationally, and internationally.

Because of the corporate relationship we have with all humanity, we share sin commonly. When a calamity befalls you, therefore, do not look for self-guilt or wonder whether or not you are still in Christ. The apostle Paul knew all about suffering firsthand. Much of his suffering was the direct result of what he was doing; but if he had connected all suffering with his own sin, he could have concluded that what he was doing was wrong. On the contrary, what he was doing was the righteousness of God. He was preaching the gospel! When he was shipwrecked, he did not interpret that as a warning not to continue his journey. He was continually in danger, sometimes from the Jews, sometimes from the Gentiles. He had trouble sleeping at night; he suffered from hunger; sometimes he did not have proper clothing (2 Corinthians 11:23-28). All of this suffering was related to sin, but not to Paul's personal sin. He was the victim, not the sinner.

Some suffering is connected to the errors of others, without any intentions of being hurtful. For instance, a person who works just for the pay, with no concern for the product he makes, may contribute to careless workmanship. The deficient product may cause a tragedy for others. Negligence on the assembly line in a factory may cause a car's brakes to fail, resulting in the death of a whole family. In fact, I personally know of a plancload of people who were killed because one bolt in the airplane had been installed upside down.

Some of our present sufferings result from decisions made generations ago. The dropping of the atomic bomb in Japan thirty years ago is still causing deformity in newborn babies. We are reaping the results in our youth now of the "permissiveness" of a decade ago. The kind of television programs we allow our small children to watch now will affect their adulthood adjustments. The drug culture will affect many generations to come, even though those unborn children did nothing wrong themselves. Multiple divorces in a family will disturb and distort attitudes and adjustments in the family for generations.

It is not enough to ask what God's will is concerning suffering and tragedies. We must also ask, "What is man's responsibility in it, individually and corporately?" At the same time, we cannot connect every act of suffering with a corresponding sin. The disciples tried to do that when they asked Jesus, "Who sinned, this man or his parents, that he was born blind?" (John 9:2; NIV). Jesus answered, "Neither."

It is also a mistake to conclude that those who suffer more severely are worse sinners. Jesus countered this idea by saying: " 'Do you think that these Galileans were worse sinners than all the other Galileans because they suffered this way? I tell you, no! But unless you repent, you too will all perish. Or those eighteen who died when the tower in Siloam fell on them—do you think they were more guilty than all the others living in Jerusalem? I tell you, no!" (Luke 13:2-5; NIV).

There are certain clear-cut consequences that we call upon ourselves because of the decisions we make. These are often the result of simply not using our common sense, and it is not correct to blame God for them or associate them with sin.

LAWS OF NATURE AND SUFFERING

God has created a marvelous world in which He has programmed many laws of nature. These laws are constant. We can and do depend upon them. Without them we could make no plans. God has built into these laws both blessings and wrath. We are blessed when we live in accordance with the laws, but we experience the wrath when we violate them. Some of what the Bible refers to as the wrath of God comes in the package of violating His natural laws.

The law of gravitation is a blessing, and we depend upon it. We could not build an airplane or a car without depending upon it. We could not put anything on the table without it. A person certainly could not wear a wig without it! But the law of gravitation becomes wrath when someone falls off a high place. Such a tragedy is not connected with a personal sin. A baby falls out of a crib and sustains a serious injury, but we cannot blame God for the tragedy. We can expect to be hurt when the laws of nature are violated, and ignorance of that law makes no difference in the results.

Sufferings are caused also by the combination of sin and the violation of the laws of nature. A drunkard (sin) causes an automobile collison (violating law of nature). A person with uncontrolled anger (sin) uses a gun to shoot another person (violating law of nature). Sin seems to find ways to do both—violate the laws of nature and cause suffering.

It is probable that diseases also are related to the violation of the laws of nature. We do not know the exact cause of many diseases, but it is my judgment that they are caused by the lack of harmony within nature. The lack of harmony is caused by the decisions of men. However, the total creation is so vast and complex that it is impossible to pinpoint with certainty a specific cause of a specific disease. We do know that there is a complex inter-dependence between man and nature. What could be causing the cancer we see all about us? Is it food that we are eating? Drugs we are taking? Could it be the sprays that we use on crops? Is it something we are doing now, or could it be something that was done or begun a generation or two before us? The question is indeed complex. Blaming God is not the answer.

MIND AND MATTER

Apart from the suffering caused by personal sin, the sin of another, the mistakes of someone else, or by violating the laws of nature, much suffering is caused by our own attitudes and thoughts about God, ourselves, others, and life itself. This type of suffering is called psychosomatic. It is no longer a secret that many people are sick because they think they are. It has been estimated that somewhere between seventy and ninety percent of all sicknesses have their source in this type of thinking.

There is certainly a relationship between mind and matter. This is seen in early childhood. A toddler hurts his finger and cries, the parent kisses the spot, and the pain and tears magically disappear. Love can heal.

A Christian woman told me about this power of love that was demonstrated in her life. Her huband had been in a coma for several days. Then one day she was told that he would die that night. She thought about her life with this man, how they had struggled to save his life, and now she contemplated how he would probably be dead by morning. She went to his side, put her arms around him, and for fifteen minutes told him how much she loved him, whispering in his ear all the endearing, sweet things she knew he would like to hear. She thought he could not even hear her; but when she finished, he was smiling. By the next morning, he was speaking. Several years later, he was sitting in the next room as she was relating this story to me.

The Bible makes it clear that our speech affects our health: "There is one whose words are like the thrusts of a sword; but the tongue of the wise brings healing" (Proverbs 12:18). "Pleasant words are like a honeycomb, sweet to the soul, and healing to the body" (16:24). "Death and life are in the power of the tongue" (18:21; RSV). "Anxiety weighs down the heart of a man, but a good word makes it glad" (12:25). "A soothing tongue is like a tree of life, but a perverse tongue crushes the spirit" (15:4).

The Bible also says our attitudes affect our health: "A kind man benefits himself, but the cruel man hurts himself" (11:17). "A tranquil heart gives live to the flesh, but passion rots the bones" (14:30).

Far more than we imagine or suspect, sickness and suffering result from our being out of harmony with God, ourselves, and others. Anxiety and anger take a great toll. God's direction for our lives has far-reaching implications, calling for selflessness, trust, love, peace, and a reordering of values. God does not give us directions just to get us to Heaven. He also wants to bring some of the heavenly life-style into our earthly existence, so that we may have abundant living.

Some doctors have suggested that medical bills among Christians could be cut at least in half, if they would exercise love and fellowship with each other more. The Bible is clear that Christian fellowship is needed for our joy to be complete (1 John 1:1-4, 7), and joy affects our health. The Bible says that our fellowship is partly for the purpose of encouraging one another, building up one another, and cheering up one another (1 Corinthians 14:3; Hebrews 10:25). It should be no mystery why we are to live with one another with kindness, gentleness, patience, forgiveness, and love, binding everything together in harmony (Colossians 3:12-16). These qualities are needed if people are to have fellowship. As a matter of fact, there is one clear case in the Bible where factions within the church were stated as the cause of the physical sicknesses and death of Christians (1 Corinthians 11:17-30).

Surely the devil is personally involved in luring us to sin and causing suffering. But why does God allow the devil to do so? Where is God and what is He doing in the midst of these calamities, while we are facing suffering and tragedy? What is His will? The next chapter will consider these questions.

lesson nine

God and Satan in Our Suffering

"God, where are You? We are hurting!"
That is not a new cry for people who have put
their trust in a God of love. The cry was heard
throughout the Bible.

THE PRESENCE OF GOD
Toward the end of the first century, when it
looked as though everything was falling in on
the Christians, God heard that same cry. Per-
secution was severe. Some Christians were
deported (Revelation 1:9), some were put in
dungeons (2:10), and others were killed
(20:4). In addition to this attack on the Christians, there were the natural calamities of
hunger and disease (6:8; 7:16). As if that were
not enough, within the church itself there
were false teachers causing internal problems. (2:2, 14, 20, 24). The Christians were
asking, "Where is our future? Where are You,
God? Don't You care? What about all those
promises You made to us: 'I'll never desert
you'; 'All things work to the good'; 'You will be
more than conquerers'? Why, God?"
The book of Revelation shows us clearly
that God and Christ know all about our problems and they care. John had a wonderful vision of Christ as well as a vision of all the

91

problems surrounding God's people. Where was Christ? He was in the midst of the people with the problems (1:13). "I'm there in the suffering with you" is our assurance.

John saw Christ clothed with a long robe and a golden girdle—the symbols of authority. Although it appears that suffering, pain, and tragedy might have the last word, they do not. Jesus Christ is on His throne. The future belongs to Him. There is no need to be afraid, for He is the first and the last (1:17). After all the smoke has cleared, Jesus will still be there in the midst of His people. To John, Jesus' feet were as burnished bronze (1:15). This is a symbol of stability. Nothing can knock Him off His throne. No one can wipe Him out. He is secure. "Behold I am alive for evermore, and I have the keys of Death and Hades" (1:18; RSV).

What does it mean to say that Jesus is "with us" in our suffering? for one thing, it means He suffers with us. We have, as Christians, a personal relationship of oneness with Him. The church is called the body of Christ, and Jesus is called the head of the body (Ephesians 1:22, 23). When the body hurts, so does the head. A Christian never experiences suffering alone. Our sufferings are Christ's sufferings, as His are to be ours (2 Corinthians 1:5; 1 Peter 4:13).

He is also with us, because we have access to His strength. His resources are ours. Because He is the Almighty one, we can be more than conquerors over whatever threatens us (Romans 8:37). "For God did not give us the spirit of timidity; He gave us a spirit of power and love and self-control" (2 Timothy 1:7).

Never are power and self-restraint more necessary than in the face of difficulty. The nearness of God is not determined by our feelings. He is there because He promised to be, and He is faithful to His promises, whether we "feel" He is there or not.

THE IMPARTIALITY OF GOD

The Christian need not worry and say, "What have I done to deserve this?" God does not use suffering, pain, and tragedy to "get even" with us for wrongdoing. We have seen already how a person may suffer as a result of these: his own sin, violating the consistent laws of nature, someone's unintentional mistakes, or someone else's sin.

Nature itself has experienced an upheaval because of man's sin, and man in return receives the consequences of that upheaval. God does not normally intervene to isolate His people from these natural consequences. "God is no respecter of persons," that is, partial. The sun shines upon all, both good and evil, and the rain falls upon all, both the good and the evil. Either can be harmful as well as helpful. Likewise impartial are natural disasters, such as tornadoes, famines, and disease, whether it be a little headache or terminal cancer. To be "in Christ" is no guarantee that we will escape crises and calamities. They will exist as long as the tempter is still alive and active among us.

THE GOODNESS OF GOD

God's goodness in the midst of our pain is apparent. First of all, pain in itself is a blessing from God. It is the warning system that something is wrong. Without the gift of pain, we would not take our hands out of the fire until too late. Without pain one would lose the use of all of the members of his body by misusing them or neglecting them. Still, this does not lessen the uncomfortableness of pain; it still hurts.

Pain is also limited and temporary. It can go only so far before our senses become numb to it. Because of God's goodness, our bodies are mortal; thus the pain in them is temporary. God will not let pain and suffering have the last word. Physical death is a God-given relief from earthly pain and pressures.

Not only has God provided an exit from earthly pain, but He has also provided an exit from eternal pain and suffering. He accomplished this in the death and resurrection of Jesus Christ. Jesus experienced for us the eternal consequences of sin. He took separation from the Father in our stead. "Surely he bore our griefs and carried our sorrows; . . . the chastening for our iniquities fell upon Him for our well-being, and with His stripes we are healed" (Isaiah 53:4, 5). Our "well-being" and "healing" are both spiritual and physical. Although the blessings begin in this life, they do not reach their fullness until that time when the perishable puts on the imperishable and the mortal puts on the immortal (1 Corinthians 15:53).

SATAN IN OUR SUFFERING

Sin continues, partly because the tempter is still active and partly because people continue to yield to him. Nature's imbalance continues to pour its threats into the experiences of all of us. The death and resurrection of Jesus did indeed defeat Satan, but he will not be finally crushed until the second coming of Christ. Although God's kingdom has come, Satan's kingdom has not departed. We are living in the overlapping of the kingdoms.

The church is engaged in a warfare with Satan's principalities and powers (Ephesians 6:12). Although Jesus has already defeated Satan, the battle wages on. Satan is like a defeated general who will not admit his defeat. He is still prowling about "like a roaring lion, seeking some one to devour" (1 Peter 5:8; RSV).

Satan is trying to defeat us on at least three battlefronts: (1) He wants us to believe that all sickness, suffering, and tragedy are the result of demon possession. If he can get us hooked on that idea, then he will get us to substitute exorcism (casting out demons) for repentance, a life of loving fellowship, and edification. We will spend more time looking at our crises than at Christ. We will spend more time exorcising than evangelizing. Satan knows that in evangelism lies his defeat, for demons cannot live in a body reconciled to the Spirit of Christ.

(2) Satan wants us to believe that our personal plights are the result of our lack of spirituality. If Satan can get us to believe that, he will succeed in getting us to doubt our status in Christ. He delights in getting us to believe that the prayer of faith will *always* heal the sick. Then when healing does not take place, we can doubt either our own faith or the faith of the church. What a masterful way to program disillusionment!

Satan is tickled beyond words when a Christian takes a verse of Scripture out of context, such as, " 'If two of you agree on earth about anything they ask, it will be done for them by my Father in heaven' " (Matthew 18:19; RSV). So what happens when two people agree that another should get well and he does not? Doubt comes. Or these verses: " 'Whatever you ask in my name, I will do it' " (John 14:13; RSV); " 'If you abide in me, . . . ask whatever you will, and it shall be done for you' " (15:7; RSV). When the healing does not take place, or when disaster still comes, we begin to doubt either our relationship with Christ or His power. Another victory for Satan!

The first quoted verse in the preceding paragraph refers only to praying for God's will to be done in the matter of disciplining a brother, and for praying for what squares with God's revealed Word and will (Matthew 18:15-35). The people praying must be in agreement, and their agreement must be in accordance with God's prior agreement as stated in verse 18, "Whatever you bind on earth will be bound in heaven, and whatever you loose on earth will be loosed in heaven" (NIV).

Binding and loosing were terms for accepting and rejecting. The original Greek does not read, "Whatever you bind or loose *shall be* loosed in Heaven," as is translated in some versions. It reads, *"Shall have been."* The idea is that the disciples should accept and reject on earth what already has been accepted and rejected in Heaven. That is, our prayers are to be in accordance with what already has been accepted or rejected in Heaven. The text does not suggest that two people can agree and pray about anything they please, and God will automatically put His stamp of approval upon the request. It suggests instead that two people know God's Word and pray in accordance with that.

The two verses from John concern prayers requesting that God use us in doing His work (14:12) and in bearing fruit (15:8).

Suffering does not indicate a lack of spirituality, or a lack of power in our prayers. Jesus experienced severe pain, which was not His only suffering. He suffered mental and emotional anguish as well as pain. We are told that He learned obedience through the things He suffered (Hebrews 5:8). Would anyone suggest He lacked spirituality? (See 1 Peter 2:20-24.)

Paul also suffered much (2 Corinthians 11:23-29). Three times he prayed that a thorn in his flesh be taken from him, but it was not (12:8, 9). He knew what it meant to be sick (Galatians 4:13). Stephen became a martyr (Acts 7:59, 60), and yet we are told that he was "full of faith and of the Holy Spirit" (Acts 6:5). Epaphroditus got sick doing the Lord's work (Philippians 2:25-30); Timothy had stomach trouble (1 Timothy 5:23). Paul left Trophimus ill at Miletus (2 Timothy 4:20). Wasn't Paul spiritual enough to pray effectively for healing?

According to tradition, Matthew was killed with a sword in Ethiopia; Mark was dragged in the streets in Alexandria; Luke was hanged in Greece. John was put in burning oil, but survived. Peter was crucified upside down;

Philip was hanged; Bartholomew was flayed; Andrew was bound to a cross and died there while preaching. Thomas was thrust through with a sword in India; Matthias was stoned and then beheaded. Barnabas was stoned; Paul was beheaded. Would we want to use these Scriptures (Matthew 18:19; John 14:13; 15:7) against them as spiritual leaders?

God never promised that spiritual people would be guarded against suffering. Not once did God promise that. Instead, He promised that we would be blessed in our suffering (Matthew 5:10-12; 2 Corinthians 1:6; Philippians 1:29; 3:10; 1 Thessalonians 2:14; 2 Timothy 2:12; 3:12; James 5:10, 11; 1 Peter 1:3-9; 2:19-24; 3:14-22; 4:1, 2, 12-19; 5:10).

(3) The third way Satan is trying to defeat us is by tempting us to do evil. When we yield, we pour alienation into God's system—person against God, person against person, person against nature, and nature against person.

Satan is shrewd. He uses both the world God created and the desire God gave us as his arena of temptation. James put it this way:

"Let no one say when he is tempted, 'I am tempted by God'; for God cannot be tempted with evil and he himself tempts no one; but each person is tempted when he is lured and enticed by his own desire. Then desire when it has conceived gives birth to sin; and sin when it is full-grown brings forth death" (1:13-15; RSV).

The devil uses our desires to lure and entice us. What a trick! Our basic desires—hunger, thirst, sex, self-preservation, etc.—are God-given and not bad in and of themselves. To satisfy those natural desires, God gave us a very good world within which those desires could be met. He gave us food to meet the desire for hunger, liquid for thirst, males and females for sex. But because God not only loves us but knows us, He also gave us commands concerning these desires. These commands serve as guardrails to protect us along the highway of life. As long as we remain within the guardrails, we can enjoy our earthly journey. He gives us the important guardrail of moderation to guide our eating and drinking to meet our hunger and thirst. He provided marriage as a guardrail to our enjoyment of sex.

Satan uses the same desires and the same world, but lures and entices us to satisfy our desires beyond God's guardrails. He says, "Eat and drink all you want. Use things just for yourself. Have sex outside of marriage if you want real fun." Satan baits the hook (lure) and it looks so good. Often it appears even logical. But we fail to see the hook inside the bait.

Satan treats us like dumb creatures. The words "lure" and "entice" were hunting and fishing terms. Christians must refuse to be treated like lower creatures that are governed by animal instinct and appetite. We are made in God's image and should behave like it.

THE VICTORIOUS ONE

In the face of both temptations to evil and the sufferings within various circumstances of life, we must realize that over against Satan is God. He still has the last word, and His promise to us is this: "No temptation has overtaken you but such as is common to man. God is faithful, and He will not let you be tempted beyond your strength, but with the temptation will also provide the way of escape, that you may be able to endure it" (1 Corinthians 10:13). Satan is like a lion on a chain, but God is holding that chain. God will never allow Satan to tempt any of us beyond our present spiritual maturity to defeat temptation.

I am confident that each day Satan tries to tempt me beyond my ability, but God says, "No!" Satan then tries again a bit closer to my level of maturity, but God still says, "No!" Those temptations are never permitted to enter into my mind. Finally Satan gets down to my level of maturity, and God says, "O.K., you can use that, Satan, because he is able in his present maturity to handle that one." That becomes the temptation which enters my thinking or experience. The moment it does, I know that I (to the degree to which I live Christ and allow Christ to live through me) am bigger than the temptation; otherwise God would not have allowed the thought or situation to arise. When I yield to the temptation, I have permitted something weaker than myself to be victorious over me. Satan is always weaker than the Christian. "He who is in you is greater than he who is in the world" (1 John 4:4; RSV). God will not keep temptations or suffering situations away from us, but He will keep those that are more powerful than we from touching us (Job 1). That is His promise. He also promises to work good out of whatever suffering circumstances come our way. The next chapter will develop this truth further.

Progress Through Suffering

Pain, sickness, and suffering are not a part of God's intention for mankind. That is clear when we consider the life in the Garden of Eden before the fall. We can also see this as we read about the activity of Jesus, who healed sicknesses and was full of compassion, and when we view Heaven with John:

"He shall wipe away every tear from their eyes, and there shall be no more death; there shall not be any mourning, or crying, or pain, for the former things have passed away. He who is sitting on the throne has said, 'Behold, I make all things new'" (Revelation 21:4, 5). God allows the built-in penalty of sin to sting, the imbalance of nature to hurt, and the schemes of Satan to test. But God has the first and the last word. The first word is His permission based upon our maturity. The last word is the good that He can work through any situation. While Satan intends to use certain circumstances to embitter us, God intends to use those same circumstances to better us.

Paul affirmed it when he said, "And we know that in all things God works for the good of those who love him" (Romans 8:28; NIV). Literally, in the Greek, we read, "God is working *with* all things *into* good for the ones who are loving God." What a promise! Circumstances are never without the accompanying activity of God who is working them into good, regardless of the possible evil intentions from the powers behind those circumstances.

PROGRESS THROUGH FAITH

We may ask, "What good is God working?" This would be impossible to ascertain, since each different situation could result in a different good. We can know only some general principles. James says that we must consider it all joy when we fall into various testings. Why? The word "testing" used in this instance refers to testing for refining purposes. It was the term used to describe the refining of precious metals through fire. "Going through the fire" was of benefit to the metals, for the fire burned off whatever was not a beneficial part of the metal. It is the same when our faith hits the fire of testing. Our faith can come out on the other side of the suffering situations stronger and more pure, because the sham and counterfeit have been burned off.

PROGRESS THROUGH EVALUATION

Suffering situations have a way of enabling us to separate what is temporary from what is eternal. Sickness reminds us that we are all temporary. Natural calamities (earthquakes, tornadoes) remind us that property and possessions are temporary. To find security or stability through it all, our eyes turn to what is lasting—God. He will never blow away or die.

God does not make suffering happen, but He does turn them into good use. The apostle Peter put it this way:

"Now for a little while you may have suffered grief in all kinds of trials. These have come so that your faith—of greater worth than gold, which perishes even though refined by fire—may be proved genuine and may result in praise, glory and honor when Jesus Christ is revealed" (1 Peter 1:6, 7; NIV).

PROGRESS THROUGH MATURITY

God also uses suffering situations to help us grow and mature spiritually. Of course, we can mature without them, but God uses the situations to speed our maturity. James said, "The testing [refining] of your faith develops endurance" (James 1:13). "Endurance" refers to remaining under or standing firm in a difficult situation; remaining under or enduring in this way produces character (Romans 5:4). Character, personal maturity, and increased trust are never gained by running away or ignoring tough circumstances. How can we measure our maturity with God if we do not walk through difficult times with Him? How can we grow if we always look for the nearest exit?

Whenever we come upon a distressing situation, we are tempted to avoid growth through testing by putting up one or more defense mechanisms. A defense mechanism is a "tool" we use to avoid facing problems squarely and handling the difficult situation. There are two broad categories of defense mechanisms: passive and violent. Both of these dodge responsible involvement.

103

To illustrate the passive defense mechanism, let us examine a common difficulty caused by marital conflict. A husband and wife are not getting along well, and one partner decides to take the passive role. This can be done by using the silent treatment (refusing to talk over the problem), or taking an exit—get out of the situation through separation or divorce. Neither of these passive roles will add to one's understanding or growth. Both bypass responsibility and fail to help the persons involved to grow in maturity.

In situations other than marital trouble, the silent approach is also used. A person will not discuss his problem with anyone. Then his imagination goes to work and builds the difficulty up until it grows out of proportion. He will withdraw into himself and will not mature. Others exit from their troubles by resigning from a job, moving out of town, or committing suicide. They cannot grow to maturity by using any of these routes.

To illustrate the violent defense mechanism, one may lash out at another person with either his lips (verbal) or his limbs (physical). Most people especially like to use this violent approach when they have been treated wrongly, for it seems to soothe their hurt feelings. To use this is to bypass meaningful interpersonal relationships with others. It feeds the narrowness of the selfish ego.

Both the passive and the violent mechanisms mean that the person draws only from his own emotional resources. He allows his life to rotate around self only. His values are centered in his ego, and he will not mature beyond his present level of selfishness.

In contrast, Jesus showed us how to handle mistreatment. He endured it; He remained under it with trust in God. After considering Jesus' example, Peter said, "To this you have been called, because Christ also suffered for you, leaving you an example, that you should follow in his steps" (1 Peter 2:21; RSV).

What was that example? He committed no sin. No deceit was found in His mouth. When He was reviled, He did not revile in return. While under suffering He uttered no threats. What did He do then? He kept trusting himself to God who judges righteously, demonstrating endurance of faith (1 Peter 2:22, 23). He maintained His fellowship and interpersonal exchange with others. He differed, but without animosity.

This is not an easy example to follow, but it is necessary for us to learn to do so in order to grow spiritually. It produces endurance, which in turn produces a more mature and stable character. Peter suggests that godliness, brotherly kindness, and love are included in this character (2 Peter 1:7). This is what Paul meant when he said, "We also rejoice in our sufferings, because we know that suffering produces perseverance; perseverance, character; and character, hope" (Romans 5:3, 4; NIV).

The word for "character" is from the same Greek root as that of "testing." Character comes out of testing. Is it possible that without testing there is little development of character? It is interesting to note that the Greek word for "glory" also comes from the same word family as "testing" and "character." In fact, one's character was referred to as one's glory. Could it be possible that, after becoming Christians, we do not mature from one degree of glory to another if we use defense mechanisms to avoid difficult situations? Paul says that by beholding the glory of the Lord "we all are being changed into his likeness from one degree of glory to another" (2 Corinthians 3:18), ie., from our own character to His. We do that as we behold and learn and follow His way of living through difficult times.

Immediately following these words, Paul affirms that he will not use any defense mechanisms to bypass difficulties which may come from being a messenger of God (4:1, 2). He does confess that difficult times have come, but they were not destructive. When he wrote, "We are afflicted" (v. 8), he used a word that described the crushing of grain or grapes. But Paul added quickly, "but not crushed; perplexed [baffled and frustrated], but are not driven to despair; persecuted [chased], but not forsaken; struck down, but not destroyed" (vv. 8, 9; RSV). Christians were at times at their wits' end, but never at their hope's end. There were times when they felt they had come to a dead end or a rock wall with no room to turn around; but there was never a time when they could not hear the rumbling of the bulldozer on the other side of the wall making a new opening.

PROGRESS THROUGH FELLOWSHIP

Through difficult situations we gain something of God's perspective and can better manifest God's patience and kindness to others. We will be better equipped to share

106

God's kind of comfort with others in their difficult times because we understand what they are thinking and feeling. We have walked with trust in God through similar situations, and can guide them as well as sympathize. This also gives us added strength.

Paul confessed that God is the Father of all comfort, "who comforts us in all our affliction, so that we may be able to comfort those who are in any affliction, with the comfort with which we ourselves are comforted by God" (2 Corinthians 1:4). In fact, he said, "If we are afflicted, it is for your comfort" (2 Corinthians 1:6; RSV). The ability to comfort people is a gift God gives to some Christians. For some, it comes through the handling of difficult times triumphantly.

What an insight! We Christians are connected to each other, for the church is a body. There is a "dominoeing" effect within Christianity. The attitudes and activities of one person can spread like cancer. A little leaven leavens a whole lump. Have you noticed how quickly the defeatist and negative attitudes spread? Some people are defeated by these poisonous attitudes and are not equipped to handle difficulties of life. Victorious, positive, and optimistic attitudes can spread also. These will equip a person to be triumphant in difficulty. How do such attitudes spread? By our actions and our speech. But we won't have much victory to spread unless we have gone through some battles ourselves. The church needs those who with faith have conquered whatever threatened them. Some of the greatest people of God have been some of those little people who have walked through difficult times with God. Their examples of triumphant faith can minister to us.

PROGRESS THROUGH HUMILITY

God also can use difficult circumstances to humble us and help us to depend upon Him. Paul sensed that he needed such dependence, and I suspect we do also (2 Corinthians 1:9). It is easy to think things are getting done just because of *me*. In the midst of prosperity, it is easy to think, "Who needs God? I can make it alone." If we get hungry, we can go to the supermarket. If we get sick, we can go to the doctor. If we lose our jobs, we can get unemployment checks. When that runs out, we can go on welfare. If a tornado hits our home, we have insurance. If the insurance doesn't cover it all, we can go to the loan companies. When we grow old, there will be social security and pensions. We can even arrange our own funerals. So, who needs God? Such pride, arrogance, and autonomy are damaging to ourselves and to the society in which we live. We need to have times in which there is no one else to turn to but God, so that these selfish qualities will be curbed, and dependence on God will be cultivated.

PROGRESS THROUGH HOPE

In discussing difficult times, Peter said, "Blessed be God and the Father of our Lord Jesus Christ, who because of His great mercy provided a way for us to be born again to a living hope, through the resurrection of Jesus Christ from the dead" (1 Peter 1:3). "Living hope" is an active hope. It does not sit around and wring its hands. It is based on evidence.

Fact produces hope and hope produces action. For instance, when you receive word that relatives are coming to visit, hope concerning that visit is produced. That hope results in preparatory activity—cleaning the house, planning the menus, and planning activities.

It is the same with our Christian hope. The resurrection is evidence that God can be victorious in tragedies, however bad they may appear. If God can bring victory out of the cross, He can be victorious in any situation. So Christians do not sit around and worry, but they plan and work for Christ.

VICTORY OR DEFEAT

While Satan can use the difficult circumstances to turn us from God, God can use them to turn us to Him. There are many ways that good can come out of troubles, but we cannot decide in advance what good will come. We cannot see what the good is, even at the present. What we can do is continue to trust that God, who has always kept His promises, will continue to do so, whether we recognize it or not. When we do realize the good that has come out of a trying situation, let us then testify about it and give God the glory for it. Remember, however, that the promise of God to make good come out of every circumstance is not for everyone, just for those who love God (Romans 8:28). For others, such circumstances cause them to turn away from God, not to Him. Their only resort is to criticize, not to comfort another; to destroy character, not to build it.

Whether we are victorious or defeated in life depends on what we hope for, how we hope

ROUTE OF DEFEAT

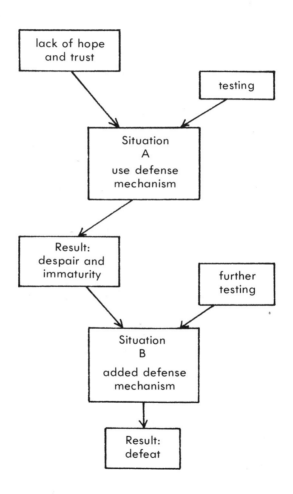

ROUTE OF VICTORY

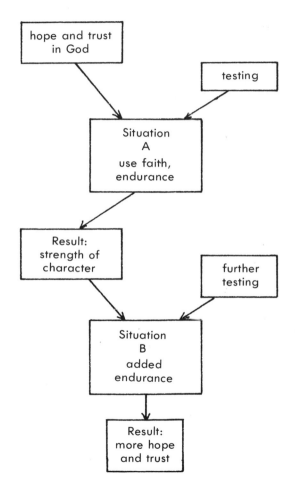

(active or passive), in whom we believe (in self or God), and what we do (endure or exit). The results of what happens in one testing situation (A) is poured into the next testing situation (B). Out of one situation, we can either have more hope and trust and love to pour into the next situation (victory), or we will have more despair and defense mechanisms to pour into it.

Of course, troublesome times will come. We shall never be free from suffering and testing. We should remember that God is working with them to bring a good result. Remember too that the sufferings of the present are not worth weighing against the glory that is to be revealed to us at the second coming of Christ (Romans 8:18). Jesus himself faced what looked like defeat, but He was victorious. Our lives are hid in Him, and His victory is ours. "Thanks be to God, who gives us the victory through our Lord Jesus Christ. Therefore, my beloved brethren, be steadfast, immovable, always abounding in the work of the Lord, knowing that in the Lord your labor is not in vain" (1 Corinthians 15:57, 58; RSV).

"For whatever is born of God overcomes the world; and this is the victory that overcomes the world, our faith" (1 John 5:4; RSV).